PLAYWR

for THEATER

FILM and

TELEVISION

Laura Shamas

808. 2

1. Playwriting
2. Authorship - Films
and television

punch
ISBN 1-55870-213-X
LC 91-19479

BETTERWAY PUBLICATIONS, INC.
WHITE HALL, VIRGINIA

Dedication: To my parents.

Published by Betterway Publications, Inc.
P.O. Box 219
Crozet, VA 22932
(804) 823-5661

Cover design by Rick Britton
Typography by Kurt H. Fischer

Library of Congress Cataloging-in-Publication Data

Shamas, Laura Annawyn
Playwriting for theater, film, and television / Laura Shamas.
    p. cm.
    Includes bibliographical references and index.
    ISBN 1-55870-213-X (pbk.) : $11.95
    1. Motion picture authorship. 2. Television authorship.
    3. Playwriting. I. Title.
PN1996.S387 1991
808.2—dc20   91-19479
                                                              CIP

Printed in the United States of America
0 9 8 7 6 5 4 3 2

Contents

Acknowledgments

Thanks to West Coast Ensemble (Los Angeles), Pepperdine University (Malibu), and the University of Colorado (Boulder); I've appreciated the opportunities to teach playwriting at these institutions. Also to the writers and students who participated — I'm grateful for your support.

My heartfelt thanks to David Rodes, Jean Korf, Clarence Major, and Joy Harjo for the guidance they've given me through the years.

And to Christopher Sergel (Dramatic Publishing Company), thanks and thanks.

Introduction:
How to Use this Book

"Play" writing has evolved significantly over the last century to include not only works for the stage but for the screen as well. Although the specifics involved in creating these forms are different, I believe that the basic dramatic writing principles — the foundation for these works — are the same for theater, film, and television.

I want to help you to write a stage play, a screenplay, or a teleplay — a wonderful, brilliant work that only you could create, that will make a lasting impression on your audience and will make you feel fulfilled.

I hope you will come to look at this book as a tool that can be used over and over again, as new ideas come to you, and as you continue to explore your interest in writing. I'm going to describe in detail the essence of good dramatic writing and the key elements involved in creating it. I've incorporated some exercises to help you develop writing muscles and to inspire you to flex them to the best of your abilities.

Like anything that's important and worth doing, it's going to be hard at times. But I will help you overcome periods of doubt and stress, and try to keep you focused on your work. I want you to finish what you start.

I'm a writer, too, and I know how lonely it can be when you begin working on a project. Fortunately, if you're working on something dramatic, you'll get to work with lots of other artists eventually (directors, actors, producers, sound and lighting designers, etc.); your job becomes quite social. But in the beginning, it takes self-discipline to get your ideas from the abyss of your brain to the glow of the computer screen. This book will keep you organized and motivated.

I will guide you through a step-by-step course to develop your ideas and put them into the dramatic form of your choice. Whether you want to write a play, teleplay, or screenplay, start at the beginning of the book and read it all the way through to get the maximum effect of this training.

I hope that you will come to think of this volume as a friendly companion on your quest to express your thoughts and talent. At times it will be an ally, then a taskmaster, later a critic, and finally, a cheering audience. You can count on thinking a lot through the whole process.

As you start your project, I recommend you keep a journal as a companion to this guide, and to record the exercises you do. It will help you release some writing tension that may come about, and at the end, you'll have a record of how you created your piece. You can use this record as a springboard to begin your next project: you'll have a specific anatomy of your creative process. You won't be afraid to start the next project — you'll know how you did it the last time and that you can do it again.

It's always exciting to start something new. I envy you. Warm up your brain and your fingers. Be brave. Write something that matters to you.

Laura Shamas
1991

1.
Why Write?

Here we are in the video age, a time when people have less time for leisure activities than ever before. That means less time for entertainment, too — less time to read, to go to the theater or films. Sometimes, it's an effort just to rent a movie or turn on the television.

This is a book about "dramatic writing," so I'm going to assume that you want to write something for the stage or screen (or you're thinking about giving it a try and wonder how it's done).

The first thing you should think about is an audience. Who's going to be interested in what you're writing and why? Visualize them. Can you write something that will motivate people to make time to see your work?

Since the competition for leisure time is so fierce these days, a respect for the audience is vital. You can show this respect by having something important to say — a driving impulse to communicate or explore something that you think is valuable to the human condition. This can be done in a comic or serious way.

If you don't have something to communicate to an audience, then why write at all (especially in these mediums)?

Many people think they can write to clarify things for themselves. Perhaps this works as a beginning impulse, but does this attitude really force you to make your ideas work creatively? Why should other people pay to see you work out your problems? If you want to make something clear, just to yourself, you might be better off strictly keeping a personal journal or writing non-fiction essays about your life. That would be a more direct, therapeutic approach.

Not to say that art isn't therapeutic for the artist, but if that's your primary goal, you're letting down your audience. As a "dramatic writer," you make a pact with the people who congregate to experience your creation in a theater or around a screen, to deliver a social experience. In theater, you are promising them a live event — one where they can laugh, cry, and appreciate whatever you've chosen to put on stage — surrounded by other people. In movie theaters, we don't promise a live experience on the screen but know that the audience will be alive (we hope). Even on television, shows are presented with "live audience" tracks that simulate this communal feeling.

I'm giving this great emphasis at the beginning of your entertainment writing venture: It is this *living quality* that separates writing for the stage and screen from prose and poetry. Stage and screen work is brought to life in three-dimensional ways in front of an audience — there's no way this cannot be recognized as a social dynamic: you (as writer) communicate with director/actors who bring your ideas to life for an audience.

With written prose (as in a novel, for example), you have a one-on-one pact with a reader. But the three-dimensional elements are in the reader's mind. You, the author, may never see this reader. You don't know where the reader reacts, and the reader reacts alone.

You may not see every audience that views your creation with stage and screen work, but you'll watch a few *houses*, I guarantee. First of all, you'll probably want to, and second, the producing powers-that-be will request that you see a few airings of your material. If people walk out, you'll see it. If they cough or sleep through your favorite scene, you'll witness it. If they love it, you'll be there to shake their hands.

We are living in an increasingly impersonal age. We have less and less significant ways to congregate together to explore the human condition. We have places of worship, schools, courts of law, and artistic platforms (concerts, theater, film, galleries, and opera), but isn't that about it? You can see that writing a script for the stage or screen is actually a very important thing to do — whether you want to admit to the responsibility or not, you *are* contributing to the social life of your audience, not to mention the cultural, aesthetic, intellectual, and political impact of your work, depending on what it's about.

Why write — if the power of your words and the potential effect your thoughts could have on society aren't recognized by you, the writer?

Some people say they write for the money. I like to get paid for my writing, too. We all need to eat. The materialistic bent of our culture today too often measures the worth of something by its monetary value — a great mistake in most artistic endeavors. But if you feel your primary mission is to make money through writing, I challenge you to write something that will sell for lots of money that does *not* communicate something to an audience. I assure you, it will not sell if it doesn't reach anyone. And once you reach someone, why not give them your best? Why not show them your most emotional ideas, your funniest notions, your most valuable thoughts?

Works that are written with a driving passion, whether you're writing a comedy, tragedy, or docudrama, are always the best. That passion is always related to a burning desire to tell a story to someone.

And that's why you should write. Human beings crave new myths. We want communal stories, just like the ones our cave-dwelling ancestors told around their campfires. We just have more sophisticated ways of telling them now. We can bring them to life, like magic, in front of the audience's eyes.

So if you have a problem you're trying to work out that's personal, or you think you could write a screenplay that's worth a million bucks, or you just know you want to write something and you want it to be good (or any combination of the above): 1) acknowledge the power of this special medium, 2) recognize you must reach an audience and think in those terms, and 3) be passionate in your endeavor. Give us your best.

And now, before you start writing, it's time to make an assessment of the market that you're attempting to compete in. Become a market analyst. There's no better way to begin writing than to attend successful creations in each of these dramatic forms. It will give you an active guidepost of what is considered "hot" right now. It will drive home the differences between these mediums and their similarities. Finally, it will make you think about entertaining audiences with your own work.

EXERCISES

1. Go to a local play that is considered a "hit." How does the play communicate ideas to the audience? What is the audience's reaction?

2. Go to a movie that's the number one box office hit at this time. How does the film communicate to the audience? What is the audience's reaction?

3. Watch a highly rated situation comedy on television. What does the episode communicate to the audience/viewer? What is the audience's reaction?

4. After watching all three forms, analyze: what are the similarities you can see in the reaction of the audience to each of these mediums? What are the differences? What did the audience like and what didn't they like? What were the "messages" in each (i.e., was something communicated)? Which form did *you* like the best? Why?

2.
Getting an Idea

Our goal in this chapter is to take the first step—you must find something to write about and make a commitment to this idea.

For whatever reasons, you have an urge to write. What do you write about? Usually, the drive to write comes from a place deep inside us; there's something that we want to explore, because of personal interest or curiosity.

Don't worry about whether your idea is "commercial" or not. Some of the most "commercial" films are popular not because of their subject matter, but because of the way in which they are told — how they communicate to an audience (as I hope you noticed in your exploration of the exercises in Chapter 1).

So, in this very important first step, *find something to write about that will hold your interest as a writer*, you're going to live with it longer than anyone else and you'll be the one who has to promote it, at least in the beginning.

It's always easier to persuade others about the value of something when you believe in it. Honesty shines through. Be true to your own intuition about subject matter and it will translate to the written page.

A common expression I've heard about getting an idea is "to write what you know." That is definitely one way to start. But you can also "write about something that you don't know"; writing can be a way to learn about something that fascinates you. There's a practical reason that I bring this up; you can receive grants to research things in order to write about them. More important, from an emotional level, you may feel a need to open up a different side of yourself, and your imagination may be just the place to start this opening process. You may know more about things than you think! So if something interests you, and you have no experience in this area, trust your initial feeling about needing to explore it.

Sometimes you'll have a general topic but you may not have a complete story to tell. That's okay, too. A fragment of an idea that's interesting to you is worth developing. You can work out the story. It's that initial spark that pulls you to the subject matter that's so crucial.

I have a series of questions that I ask myself before committing to a specific idea:

1. Does this idea promote behavior that I wish to celebrate? Or does this idea force examination of behavior that I'm against? Celebrating or protesting behavior guarantees a passionate bent, so if I've responded "yes" to either question, I consider that a good sign.

2. Has anyone written a work on this idea before? If so, what will I do that is different? If I have no knowledge of a work on this subject, and I'm interested in it, it's a big plus for me. But even it's been written about for thousands of years, if I have a "new" slant on the issue, I know it's worth exploring.

3. Would I want to see this performed? If I can honestly say that as an audience member, I'd love to see a work on this subject, then that also inspires me to finish it. But if I wouldn't want to see it, why should I expect others to want to? So if I'm not eager to watch it, I admit to myself that it's probably not smart to spend time writing it.

In the next few pages, I'm going to detail a few processes that will help you get an idea. I hope you come up with several. After finding these ideas, it's important to make a commitment.

Commitment is a very serious part of the writing experience. Some say it takes seven years to launch the average play, from inception to the stage. Others say you can expect at least three years for film if you're lucky enough to sell one. In recent times, there are famous blockbusters that took seven to ten years to launch. Is a commitment to a writing idea the same as a commitment to marriage? It may be stretching the analogy, but indeed, if you want your idea to reach fruition, your passion for it may last longer than some relationships you've had.

You need to be able to live with your idea for a long time.

One of the most destructive things beginning writers do is to start one idea, then another, then another, out of frustration. Giving up is a last resort; if you never finish what you start, you'll never know if it works or not. Don't be flighty or whimsical: find an idea that you believe in, that you want to make part of your life, that can grow with you.

Here are a few ways you can find ideas that you can make a commitment to:

SELF-EXAMINATION

Think about your life. What are your problems? What are your strengths? What do you really think about? What do you care about? Do you daydream? What would you change about your life if you could?

If there were a movie about your life, with you as the leading character, what would be the story? Write down several issues that come to mind about your life. Who are the most interesting people that you know? How have they affected you? What is it in their characters that you find intriguing? What are your favorite expressions? How do you speak? Does your speech reflect a certain region of the country? An education level? Unique life experiences? What is it about your appearance and behavior that is unique?

How do others view you? Are you a leader? A follower? Where do you fit in your family? What is your family like? Jot down short responses to these questions; there are concepts to explore in your answers to each question. These are also universal topic areas that affect everyone. Is there one in particular to which you wrote a longer response?

OBSERVATION

Observe the world around you. What is it that fascinates you the most about the world today? What do you think is happening to the human race? No matter how many great writers have lived and died before you've taken up the art of writing, you are living at a unique point in time. You have the chance to offer observations of the world that have never been expressed before. If we could publish a book called "The World According to _____ (fill your name in here)" what would it be about? What do we need? What do we have? What are the five most crucial issues affecting human beings today, in your opinion? What public institutions would you call attention to? What about government? What about education? What about world politics? Spirituality? The current job market? The socialization process? What values do you see in the world that you'd like to applaud? What values would you like to abolish? What institutions or figures best represent these values? Jot down answers to these questions; these are things you care about that you could impart to others — from your own unique standpoint.

If you felt apathetic to all of the above questions, and don't have another idea in mind, you may not be ready to write just yet; you may not have the impulse to communicate.

If you felt that reading and answering the above questions got your juices going, try the following exercises for further stimulation.

EXERCISES

1. Read your daily local newspaper for one week. Cut the five most interesting things out of it each day (no matter what section it's from — even the classified ads count!) and put them into a file. At the end of the week, you'll have a record of thirty-five things that interest you. Eliminate all but the five most fascinating ones, and rank them in order of your interest. Now you have five possibilities to explore.

2. Keep a dream diary for one week. Every morning, as soon as you wake up, before talking to anyone or taking a shower, etc., copy down any images from your night's sleep into a journal. Even if it seems crazy, write it down as quickly as possible and put it away. Do not review it on a daily basis. But at the end of the week, look at it. You'll have several entries that should be full of unique symbols and storylines: Are any of these things you'd like to expand? What is your subconscious mind working on all night? Can you actualize it?

3. We all have favorite memories. Pick out a special event in your life and write down everything you can recall about it: the way you felt, what you smelled, what you heard, and what you saw. Who was there? What happened? Did it make you feel good to remember it? Why is this memory so important to you? Could you build a story around this scene?

3.
Imagine an Audience

You've got an idea now (or perhaps several!) that you're ready to make a commitment to. We discussed the importance of audience in the first chapter; now that you've decided what to write about, it's time to think more specifically about what an audience wants and how they receive ideas. This forethought will save many steps later on.

Have you ever been disappointed by a theatrical experience? Someone has told you how good a film was, and you saw it and thought, so what? Obviously, any judgment of an artistic work is "subjective"; even a critic has just "one person's opinion." So one person's value of art will never be exactly shared by another.

But when you have a group of people seated together experiencing a performance, they aren't offering their opinions yet. They are still involved in the act of receiving the work. You can get strong information about how writing is being received by watching how an audience behaves during a performance.

The reason they've gathered to watch this event is that they've heard something about it — through either advertising or word of mouth. Therefore, they have certain expectations. What do they want exactly?

Obviously, they've paid money for some sense of professionalism. On the most basic level, this professionalism should include the portrayal of some *events*, presented on the stage or screen, *acted out by characters, with a purpose*. This usually includes a *transformation* of a leading character. If the audience senses that there is a random or incomplete quality to what they're watching, this disappoints them. If a work doesn't seem to be about anything, or is about too many things, this disappoints them. Clarity, purpose, and focus will involve an audience, no matter what their individual aesthetic judgments may be.

We are a visually-oriented society. In a general sense, the more visual elements you can conjure up, the more the audience will respond. As a wordsmith, no one loves language more than I do. However, if beautiful words are not linked to action, it seems more like poetry than dramatic writing. Invent spectacle; by that I mean, in every scene you write, paint a picture with actions. Match spectacle with spectacular dialogue. This holds true no matter what you're writing: stage, screen, or television. Behavior should be primary, linked to crafted dialogue. Give an audience something to watch.

Reading an audience is a skill that all dramatic writers must acquire. It doesn't matter whose work it is, yours or someone else's, you can see the correlation between author and audience by observing any play or film in progress. Barring any violent etiquette problems, you can watch the behavior of the "houses" and get a feel for where they're uninvolved. Of course, if they're asleep, talking, or coughing, they're not interested. If they walk in and out a lot, they're really not interested.

At every play and film you attend, notice: Are there places where the audience is clearly bored? What's happening at this time on the stage or screen? Are there places where everyone laughs? What makes one hundred people laugh at the same time? Are there lots of people crying at the same point? Why?

Develop a sense of how to keep an audience entertained and involved (notice I haven't used the word "pleased"). This should become part of your second nature; as we become more technically engrossed in the craft of dramatic writing, it will be easy to lose sight of the audience. But you can't. Imagine them, sitting there, as three-dimensional as you want your characters to be. Imagine them laughing when you have a funny line, and gasping at a shocking point in your story.

Believe me, the rewards of audience response to a living writer are enormous. When they feel what you're trying to communicate, it's sensational. Be cognizant of them; be ready for them. It is your goal to reach them.

One of the differences between audience expectations in watching a play, film, or television show is active versus passive viewing. In a play, because of the totally live experience and often formal social arena, we are extremely "active" in our viewing. At intermission, the lights come up and we know who is seated around us. We're aware of who is in front of us and what they're wearing. Ticket prices are fairly high. The combination of these elements makes a theater house try to keep up with the play; the incentives are high. This is good news for the playwright.

At a movie, it is more casual, and because the presentation is not live, the average viewer is a bit more passive. People miss parts while at the concession stand or while they're in the bathroom. They know the movie will be shown again, exactly the same way it was before (or in a few months they can rent it). It wasn't very expensive. If you do rent it, you can stop it anytime you want. This causes less commitment from the audience. The writer should be aware of this shift; your crucial points must be made in striking ways to guarantee complete attention.

We've gotten used to watching television while doing a million different things: eating, ironing, homework, etc. Television is the most passively viewed form of the three. Additionally, you've got commercials that will interrupt and possibly discourage a viewer from staying with your show. You must rivet the audience and also realize the amount of information that you can impart in a single show will be much more limited than in the other forms. How can the audience absorb much with all these obstacles to compete for their attention?

I strongly advise you to base the scope of your idea on the form in which you wish to write.

Now that you have specific information about audience expectations, from clarity of purpose to visual awareness, and the different kinds of attention you can expect from a "house," let's work on developing your audience-reading sensibility.

EXERCISES

1. Watch an audience in a theater. Watch an audience in a movie theater. Watch a few friends or family members watching television. What are the differences? Were there active versus passive viewing habits?

2. Before you go to see a play or movie, write down what you're hoping for — in every possible sense. Are you hoping you'll run into people that you know there? Are you hoping for a good laugh? Are you hoping to see your favorite star or a subject that you love? Are you expecting your life to be enhanced in any way? See the film or drama. Immediately afterwards, write down how you feel. What did you get out of the experience? Were your expectations met? Why or why not?

4.
Different Genres, Different Effects

Now that you have this great idea brewing in your head, you're probably eager to get on with the writing process. A note of caution: The more groundwork you can lay during the fermentation period, the better your final product will be. To this end, we're going to examine the power of genre and tone in an effort to help you decide which medium your idea would work best in, and what tone to use.

What is the best platform for your idea — a stage, a movie screen, or a television screen? These are the three forms of dramatic writing today.

This is a tough decision, one that will shape the structure of your story. Each medium has its own limitations and strengths. In terms of monetary compensation, theater pays less well than film or television, if you're thinking along those lines. As you read my general descriptions below, continue to think about your idea. Where would it fit the best?

STAGE

Works for the stage these days fall into three categories: full-length plays, one-act plays, and musicals.

A full-length play is often a two-act play with one intermission or a ninety-minute play with no intermission. Very few three-act plays are produced anymore; many producers feel audiences have developed a shortened attention span with the advent of television. Musicals are sometimes written now without librettos or stories, based more on concept. Of course, they also involve the creation of songs and music.

The next statement I'm going to make is from a relatively new school of thought (and certainly not original to me); ironically, this has come about through theater's competition for film/television audiences. In general, due to the rising influence of film and television, *a work for the stage must go beyond realism in its tone and treatment of subject matter.* In other words, if you wish to write a realistic domestic tragedy, you would be better off showing it on film. The camera can give close-ups; on stage there is no way to show minute detail.

In order for a play to be "theatrical," it is essential to move into a larger-than-life, almost mythic mindset on the part of the writer. I'm not saying realistic plays don't work anymore. What I am suggesting is that a playwright these days faces a very sophisticated audience; patrons go to the theater for a social experience, as mentioned previously. But they also expect a play to do exciting things that film/television does not. A live performance is one aspect of this. Additionally, when a play tells a story in a way that film/television cannot, it is even more exciting.

What do I mean? Introduce larger-than-life, or surreal, or absurdist elements; use your imagination to expand the stage picture you're creating. Actively seek symbols to put into your visuals. If you were writing a domestic tragedy, and you decided you *had* to write it for the stage, I'd advise you to take it out of the realistic vein and into some heightened exaggeration of the condition. Maybe your story is about a wife who is overwhelmed with domestic work; instead of having a standard, realistic set with ordinary furniture, perhaps the set is oversized, with huge dirty dishes waiting on an enlarged sink.

A few years ago, I wanted to write a play about a very serious subject: rape. However, I knew there were lots of realistic plays that had already been written about it. I wanted to depict it in a way I hadn't seen in the theater: through symbols and a bit of humor to balance the tough nature of the subject matter. But I wanted to allow the audience to feel what it was like from a theatrical perspective. In my play, *Telling Time*, the woman who is raped is a children's storyteller at a local library. At the beginning of the play, which starts after the rape, she sees all the important people in her life as characters from children's books; her distortions are a sign of her inner wounds. Her mother is the Red Queen from *Alice in Wonderland*, her best friend is Snow White, her boyfriend is a pirate from *Treasure Island*, and her gynecologist is Glinda the Good Witch from *The Wizard of Oz*. There are some inherent humorous possibilities there; but moreover, it was theatrical. As the storyteller got better, the people around her began to appear in regular clothes. There were technical elements that augmented this surrealistic tone (sound, lights, props, etc.) as well. But it was my decision from the beginning to put the play beyond a realistic vein.

I'm not strictly advocating "weird" or "bizarre" perspectives for theater. But I am prescribing an approach that I firmly believe to be true; fewer people go to the theater now than attend movies, so you must deliver spectacle. If you feel you can make a realistic domestic tragedy a visual spectacle, then do it, by all means. But think big.

Theater traditionally has delivered moments of catharsis for the audience: a point where everyone does laugh or cry at that one big climax. Because of this, if your story idea has lots of emotional impact that could be enhanced through live presentation, theater may be the medium for it. Can you tell your story in 85 to 95 pages?

That's the average length of a full-length play. If you think you can tell it in 30 to 40 pages, then you have a one-act play.

Do you think your story has five to seven characters, and one or two locations? Again, a good prospect for theater. Since plays are increasingly expensive to produce, small casts with one or two sets are more likely to get produced than large-cast, multi-scened shows.

You can see that it gets increasingly difficult to deliver spectacle with these budgetary constraints, but modern playwrights must adapt, creatively.

FILM

Would you prefer that your story evolve in a realistic vein? Can you see the necessity of close-ups to tell your story? Do you have many different locations and many different characters?

Can you tell your story in 120 pages? That is the average length of a screenplay, although comedies are a little shorter. Can your story roughly fit into a structure with a beginning, a middle, and an end, since film traditionally uses a modern version of a first, second, and third act form? If so, film would suit it best. (At this time there is some crossover between films, television movies-of-the-week, and miniseries, so if you aspire to write one of those, approach it from a film standpoint at this point in the process.)

Does it have the possibility of sub-plot, a concurring storyline that will echo the primary story idea?

If it fills these very general descriptions, then your idea would best be served in the cinema medium.

TELEVISION

Is there a show on the air that you watch regularly, that you know intimately, that you feel your story could enhance? If so, then you know how long it should be, and the characters are already established for you. You actually have a strong framework to work with: a half-hour or hour-long format.

There are usually two storylines that run through these formats, the A plot and the B plot. Do you have both possibilities? If the show is a half-hour, can it be divided into two parts and a tag (short scene)? In an hour, can you make it four parts and a tag? (If you thought your idea might serve as the basis for a new show, as in a pilot, you should know that pilot ideas are normally accepted only from established television writers with proven track records.)

Now you have an overall idea of the basic characteristics of each form. Of course, just because you choose to start writing your idea as a film doesn't mean you can't revise it as a play. It's the idea you've made this commitment to, not the medium!

TONE

Tone is another writing element that can serve your idea, and a decision at the beginning about tone can save future rewrites.

A comedy is a story that is told with humor, with a leading character who undergoes a transformation. Usually, this has a happy ending.

A tragedy is a story with a leading character with some kind of fatal flaw or weakness; this results in a disastrous ending, usually death or great loss.

These days, we've got mixtures of both, and hybrids of all kinds. We've got tragicomedies (one part is relatively sad, the ending is happy), dramadies (happy/sad combo), docudramas (a documentary feel), black comedies (bad things happen but it's so bad that it's hilarious), satires (vices are held up to ridicule), absurdism (human condition is irrational and silly), surrealism (interpretation of the unconscious), etc. You can create your own tone, too.

Tone is a very powerful tool for a writer. It can allow you to explore potentially threatening ideas in a non- threatening way; comedy often contains a serious message that is easier to receive because it's delivered through laughs. Using absurdism or surrealism can relieve the intensity of your piece as well, although as a rule, these work far better in theater than in film or television. Decide what tone you want to use to tell your story, and work to maintain it as you begin your writing process.

EXERCISES

1. Think of a one-line story idea. Write it in a few paragraphs as a comedy. Write it in a few paragraphs as a serious piece. Compare the results. See how tone may affect the end result?

2. Watch a non-realistic play. Then watch a realistic film and finally, a television show. What is the emotional impact of each? What details do you remember from them? Analyze the way the stories were told. How did cameras affect the way you received the story?

3. Go see a funny movie. Can you define its message? Was it "serious"? Were there serious moments in it? Go see a serious movie. Can you define its message? Were there funny moments in it? Analyze the balance of contrasting tones in each. What conclusions can you draw about the balance of tones?

5.
Creating Characters

Now we come to the fun part — working on the nuts and bolts of developing your idea; we're starting on the step-by-step process to creating your work.

THE FIRST STEP

I believe that once you have a general story/germ of an idea, the next step in developing it is choosing the characters that are going to make it breathe and will bring it to life.

It is an old and honored theory, dating back to Aristotle, that character and action are inextricably bound together, that you cannot separate one from the other.

Once you have an idea, some sort of action is inherent in it; now you must join characters to this plan of action: the two must mesh.

It is the behavior of your characters that will be viewed by the audience. So now your work becomes similar to a detective's: You start to fit together clues of your character's life — pieces, fragments — so that by the end, we see the whole person, the big picture.

In order to develop your story, you'll need to choose characters to fit the following story positions: *protagonist* (the leading character, the one who is changed by the end of your work), *allies* (the support system of your protagonist), *antagonist* (villain, if you have one), *secondary characters* (additional characters who participate in the story).

PROTAGONIST

The protagonist is the hardest character to create. Once you figure out who is to lead your grand design, the other elements fall into place like pieces of a puzzle.

I'm sure you're thinking, "Hey, wait a minute. I barely have a story idea. And I'm not sure how much action is in it. Now you expect me to be able to describe a protagonist?" Not quite.

I've prepared a little something for you to complete, after which I think you *will* know more about this leading character. If you don't know the answer to some questions, that's okay. Make some response (even "I don't know"). But be creative; follow your whim/intuition. Let this inspire you as fill it out. Make a photocopy of the form so you can use it again.

Protagonist Questionnaire

1. Fill in a brief description of your story: _____

_____

_____

_____

2. In order to bring this to life, should your protagonist be a _____male or a _____female? (Check one) Why? _____

_____

3. What part of the country is your protagonist from?_____

_____

Why? _____

4. What city/town does your protagonist live in at the beginning of your story?_____

How did he/she end up there? _____

_____

_____

5. How old is your protagonist? _____

Why? _____

6. What does your protagonist do for a living? _____

Does your protagonist enjoy this job? _____

Why or why not? _____

How much money does your protagonist earn? _____

Is this enough for your protagonist?_____

Why or why not? _____

7. What is the education level of your protagonist? _____

Did your protagonist do well in school? _____ If so, why?

If not, why not?_____

8. Is your protagonist married? _____Why or why not?

_____

Does your protagonist have a family?_____

Who are they? _____

9. Where does your protagonist live — an apartment? House? Mobile home? _____ The street? _____ Why? _____

10. Does your protagonist own a car? _____? Why or why not? _____

11. Has your protagonist ever been to a psychiatrist? _____ Why or why not? _____

_____

12. What does your protagonist look like? _____

_____

_____

13. What does your protagonist weigh? How tall is he/she?

_____

14. What is your protagonist's favorite outfit? _____

_____

15. Is your protagonist religious? If so, what affiliation? _____ If not, why not? _____

_____

16. Is your protagonist political? If so, what party/causes?

_____

If not, why not? _____

17. What does your protagonist do for fun? _____

_____

Why? _____

18. What is your protagonist's secret dream? _____

_____

Why? _____

19. What is your protagonist's deepest fear? _____

_____

Why? _____

20. What is your protagonist's sex life like? _____

_____

Why? _____

21. What issues would make your protagonist take a heroic stand? _____ Why? _____

22. What is your protagonist's chief goal in life? _____

_____

Why? _____

23. Will your protagonist achieve this goal?_____
Why or why not? _____

_____

24. How was your protagonist born? _____

_____

25. How will your protagonist die? _____

_____

Congratulations. You have the beginnings of a professional, psychological, and social profile of your leading character. Any questions that you didn't answer are obviously points for further thought.

One big thing you don't have yet is a name for this character.

Names are definitive labels that your characters will live with. The audience will identify your leading character by the sound of this character's name. Pick a name that you like the sound of. Say it out loud several times. If it works, I urge you to look up what this name means, either in a dictionary or a baby-naming book — somewhere you can find the meaning of the roots: a little etymology never hurt any author.

I am not suggesting that you pick a name based solely on the meaning of the name. But if the sound and meaning work in tandem, it does give double impact to your character's identity.

Once I was working on a script called *Trance Dance*. I knew I wanted to work with the name "Flamenca." I didn't know why; I knew it was a name I'd never used in anything else and I really liked the sound of it. In my script, Flamenca is a young woman who discovers she has psychic ability. After I'd plowed through nearly seventy pages of the first draft, I looked up the root "flamen" in the dictionary. Its Latin root meant "seer, magician." This made me feel good — the name worked on a couple of levels.

Now is the time to name your protagonist.

You should feel exhausted: it's mental labor.

You must learn everything about your leading character, including the answers on the questionnaire, and beyond. Why must you do this? So you will know how your character will act. As the creator of this new being, you will need to justify every action your protagonist makes (and this character will be very active — it's going to drive the action of your script!).

Complete History of Protagonist

Write a complete three-page history of this new creature, your protagonist. If you don't know his or her story, no one will. You may not use all this information in your first draft or in any draft. However, it gives you a solid base to refer to as you take your character through the paces. Start at birth and write it to the point at which your story will begin. Again, be creative. Describe everything and attempt to answer why your character's life is this way. Examine behavior; look at cause and effect. Do limit yourself to three pages.

CHARACTER FILE

When you finish this biography, get a folder and put this in it. Label the folder "Characters." As you complete the other, shorter bios of the allies and antagonist, put the pages in this folder. It will become your own personal "Who's Who," a history of the people in your script. You are creating your own reference/research material; it will make you confident in your knowledge of the world of your work.

ARRANGEMENT OF THE ALLIES AND ANTAGONIST

You probably want to add characters that will round out what you consider weak sides of your main personage. Character variety is important, and that's a good instinct to have. If your character is a straight-laced businessman, you're probably already dreaming of the wacky female sidekick you want to have as his assistant, to liven things up.

But many beginning writers miss the fact that their protagonist is further defined by the company that he/she keeps. Think about your own life for a minute: Are your friends representative of your values? Maybe not exactly, but isn't there a correlation? Who are the people you strongly dislike? Why do you dislike them? Does your dislike of these people point up more about your morals and values? The same will be true of your main character and his/her relationship to those in the world of your script.

This process is called *character arrangement.* So in addition to variety, plot your other characters in a manner that further defines your protagonist and extends the possibility of action.

Clearly, the allies and antagonist in your story have different functions.

Allies, or the support system of your leading character, echo lesser characteristics of the star of your piece, things that you may not want to say directly. You can see this in some very famous, successful works for the stage and screen; you should not be afraid to try it in your own work. Allies underscore the inner core of your protagonist; perhaps spiritual, emotional, or even intellectual values held by your leading character. An ally may be a friend, family member, co-worker, etc., — anyone who provides a social, systematic framework for your hero or heroine to come back to safely.

In Wendy Wasserstein's play, *The Heidi Chronicles*, which won the 1989 Pulitzer Prize and Tony Award for best play, the protagonist, Heidi, an art professor, has a close friend named Peter Patrone. He is a prominent New York pediatrician; he helps many children. Although Heidi works with students, she longs for a direct connection — to people and to posterity. Near the end of the play, Heidi visits Peter in the ward of his hospital; she brings donations for his child-patients. In the next and final scene, the audience learns that Heidi has adopted a child. Clearly, her ally, Peter, has values that Heidi has; he realized them in a different way. Heidi's desire for children is indirectly stated through her association with Peter.

There are two classic film examples that illustrate how allies can define a leading character: *The Wizard of Oz* and *Star Wars.* In *The Wizard of Oz*, Dorothy starts to hang around the Scarecrow, the Tin Woodsman, and the Cowardly Lion (not to mention Toto!). All three characters represent things that Dorothy ends up having, through her various adventures: a brain, a heart, courage. Because these allies want these things so much, we know that Dorothy does, too.

In *Star Wars*, Han Solo, Chewbacca, R2D2, and C3PO help define who Luke Skywalker really is. Han is a cavalier adventurer, Chewbacca a primal, physical force. R2D2 represents steadiness and C3PO shows intelligence, often mixed with neurosis. All these traits are part of Luke's character and evolution.

Antagonists, or opponents, clearly define your protagonist by what he/she is *not*. You may not have an idea right now for a villain in your story. That's fine; many plays these days do not have them, although most films do.

(We'll specifically examine this in Chapter 10.) However, you should recognize that an antagonist does provide built-in action for your protagonist; by opposing a villain, your protagonist is given something to act upon/against, etc.

Another writing mistake novice dramatic writers make is to give cartoonish bad-guy qualities to villains. The more three-dimensional and human you make an antagonist, the more clearly your protagonist is defined. Anybody, any leading character, can be against a dirty, no-good, rotten murderer. But if you know that the murderer was killing in retribution for something that happened to his kind mother, and his mother was killed by an even more evil person, suddenly there's further interest in what your protagonist is going to do to this antagonist. The audience will make an emotional investment.

In general, it's more clear if there's a central antagonist to match the central protagonist, although the antagonist certainly may have allies of his/her own in the entourage. If you don't have a spot for an antagonist in your story, if you're writing a film, you might want to rethink your idea to include such a character.

Names for your allies and antagonist are very important. You don't want to use any names that are similar to your protagonist's name. Differentiate in sound and meaning. Vary them syllabically, too.

Biographies of Allies and Antagonist

Write a one-page complete history of each of the allies and of the antagonist in your script. Name them. Obviously, the questions on the protagonist's questionnaire are starting points for these descriptions as well. You will have several new reference sheets to add to the character file.

SECONDARY CHARACTERS

Of course, there are other important characters necessary to tell your story. These characters fall into the "secondary" category; this does not mean that they are not important. These characters live in the same world that your protagonist does and are somehow involved in the action of the storyline. For now, write a one-paragraph physical description of these characters; some of these may be fleshed out further at a later date. These may be characters involved in a sub-plot or in the main plot (although I don't expect you to know the plots entirely at this point). These should not be extras—characters that will end up with just minutes of stage or screen time; these are characters in your story at least one-fourth of the time. Make sure their names have variety and meaning as well.

Bios of Secondary Characters

Write a paragraph of biographical description of every secondary character that is included in your protagonist's world. You may again base it on primary questions in the Protagonist's Questionnaire.

And now for a moment of euphoria. You should have the completed Character File in your hands. Flip through it. These people will be walking through your world. You've created them for a reason. Next we'll figure out where to put them.

EXERCISES

Review of exercises in this section:

1. Protagonist Questionnaire.

2. Character File: Complete three-page history of your leading character. One-page histories of allies and antagonist. Paragraphs of secondary characters.

FURTHER BEHAVIOR EXERCISES

The ability to create character can be greatly enhanced by watching the way people behave and recording your observations.

1. People-watching is a fine way to start as long as you (a) go to a public place where you can sit for two hours and (b) bring writing materials to record descriptions of all the people who catch your attention. Describe what they wear, how they smell, the tenor of their voices, the color of their eyes, as well as speculation about what they do for a living, why they're in the same place you are.

2. Take a bus ride. Make notes about people of interest you notice on the bus. This is a great exercise because you can tell who is going somewhere in a hurry (action!) and who is in a leisurely mode. Who is polite? Who is rude?

3. Go to a place of worship. Observe the way people behave when they're trying to put their best foot forward in a sacred place. What changes in their behavior? Their dress? Their demeanor? Take a few notes, discreetly, immediately after a visit.

4. Imagine your protagonist's life for one day. Write a complete description of your character's behavior from dawn until dusk. Don't leave out anything. What is a typical day in the life of your leading character like?

6.
Setting

I'm sure you have a rough idea of where your script will take place, based on your Character File. You are creating an arena, a world for your people to inhabit, a perfect platform for your story. It's time to focus on a general setting, and to get a rough idea of where individual scenes will take place. As you outline the action of your story in the next chapter, it is crucial that you keep the following points about setting in mind.

A SPECIAL AND SPECIFIC PLACE

The world of your script must be special; by that I don't mean it has to be one-of-a-kind or fantastic, although it may have those qualities. It has to allow the audience to suspend their disbelief; they're not just watching a bunch of paid actors move across fake sets. They've come to a world, your world. It must be specifically described, and three-dimensional; only then will an audience accept it as a place where characters live. So no matter whether your setting is realistic or whimsical, true or fictional, you must create as many details as possible to bring it to life.

Here are some basic questions that can help you start to develop a sense of setting:

- Where does your protagonist live?
- What part of the country?
- What is the air like there?
- What is the weather like?
- What is the terrain?
- What is the population?
- Where does your protagonist work or enact his/her main activities?
- Where is your protagonist's favorite recreational site?
- Where does your protagonist like to drive?

SPECTACLE ELEMENTS

Whether you're writing a stage or screen manuscript, part of your ability to create a visual spectacle will be based on setting. Think of it as a canvas upon which you must paint. You must create places that are visually exciting, for one reason or another. Remember how we recognized that audiences are visually oriented? The setting is the foundation of the spectacle you will create. It should be mesmerizing in its own right, even more so with fascinating characters living in it.

LIMITATIONS OF LOCALE

If you're writing a play, you will be limited to one or two sets, as we discussed previously, due to budgetary restraints. (Note: There are ways to show multiple settings on stage with a "cinematic approach"; you use lights, sound, and minimal set pieces to suggest a variety of locales. But unless this epic scope fits your play, you probably will have to limit your locales to one or two.)

Therefore, your setting will be vitally important in order to create a stage picture. In television, sets will be established by the type of show you're writing. Even in film, where you have the luxury of shorter scenes and different locations, it's crucial to keep the different locales to the absolute fewest (also for budgetary purposes).

So take time to find the special place: it's going to have to serve you through your entire script.

ACTION ORIENTATION

Whatever action will occur in your script will occur in these settings. Think about action. I've seen many first-time dramatic writers make the fatal mistake of setting scenes in restrictive environments, where very little movement is possible, and actors have nothing to work with.

When we start writing scenes, you'll be forced to summarize the action that will take place in each section. Save yourself some misery by addressing the issue of action now.

Give the characters an environment where something can happen.

Of course, there are fantastic writers who could make an audience believe that anything can happen, in any setting, as Jean-Paul Sartre does in *No Exit* — giving us a view of hell in a room with no doors. If you are one of those people, I admire you. However, for most of us, the issue of setting/action can make the difference between a static scene and an exciting one. If you give your characters an arena to work in, they'll have something to do. If you box them in, they'll suffocate.

SETTING AS METAPHOR

My favorite writers make the setting a symbolic element of their scripts, as well as a realistic one. In other words, where the action takes place is also a symbol for what's going on in your protagonist's life.

In a published play of mine called *Living Doll*, I wrote about a woman, Rose, who had Alzheimer's Disease. Her children must come to grips with her failing health, painful as it is, and place her in special care. I created her as a woman who ran a doll-repair hospital in her home; the stage was filled with fragments of broken toys. This was my way of using setting as metaphor. This represented the state of Rose's mind. It was a realistic setting, too, although an unusual one.

If you can find ways to manifest a metaphoric setting visually, the audience will have a double view of your play — on both conscious and subconscious levels. This is a powerful and sophisticated use of setting. I encourage you to try it.

Good luck in creating your own special world. Keep these five principles in mind as you continue with the writing process.

EXERCISES

1. Try your hand at describing different sorts of landscapes. Write a one-paragraph description of the following: a desert, a mountain town, a golf course, a downtown office in a major city, a bomb shelter, heaven, a jail cell.

2. Off the top of your head, jot down five action-verbs (for example, "sail, ski, rotate, shoot, climb"). Number them 1 to 5. Write one paragraph for each of the verbs, creating a setting in which each activity occurs, for five paragraphs total.

3. Imagine a place you've never been. Open an atlas, if you're stuck, or the travel section of a newspaper, and pick a place that you find exotic and mysterious, and that you've never been to. Write a paragraph description of it.

4. Describe where you are right now, in one paragraph. Make it as detailed as possible.

5. Compare Numbers 3 and 4. What are the merits of each? Which is more specific? Which is more general?

7.
Story

Story. You know a good one when you see one or hear one. I'm sure you have an opinion of what elements make up a good story. But we're going to master the technical areas of the craft, in a formal sense; and these elements are essential to the creation of story.

HOW TO TELL A STORY

First, we'll look at the basic, traditional elements of telling a story — the arc of a plot. You've got to know the rules before you break them. If you have no context to work in, you'll have no reason to part with tradition (if you ever choose to do so)! A solid, working knowledge of the basics of dramatic storytelling is an excellent foundation for all writing.

ACTION POINT/EXPOSITION

You may have heard the expression, "A good story has a beginning, a middle, and an end." Not so in dramatic writing. Your story has a beginning, but you don't show it. You may start writing your story at the beginning, but I'll urge you to throw away your first ten to twenty pages. A good story starts at a point of action, a place where your protagonist is about to do something. On Diagram #1 (page 42), this is labeled "Action Point." Your protagonist is involved in some sort of activity at the beginning that will define him/her and propel your story forward.

This necessary definition is called "Exposition." In times gone by, audiences were used to hearing a "set-up" at the beginning of a script; in other words, some character spent a great deal of time telling the history or back story of what happened previously. Sometimes this was done by someone speaking into a phone or talking to a less important figure in the script.

41

Those times are over. These days, the audience is so action-oriented that writers must start their scripts with action and find a way to tell something about the leading character's world and background all in one fell swoop. It's very exciting to watch; "actions speak louder than words."

If a script begins with an off-duty policeman saving someone's life in an airport as he awaits his estranged wife's airplane, you know something about the back story and the leading character in one swift movement.

SERIES OF CONFLICT AND ACTION SEQUENCES

Anytime your main character acts, the resulting action will introduce a new atmosphere in your main character's life.

Change is the natural course of our world. Nothing ever remains the same. This is reflected in traditional plot structure as well. Whatever the new atmosphere that results for your character, you must present him/her with another obstacle, another event, another circumstance, something to act upon again, something that induces the growth and knowledge that are needed in order to attain a final goal (see Diagram #1).

This pattern is repeated over and over again, and it's called "Rising Action." Again and again, there is an obstacle that is faced by your protagonist, until finally, after several smaller conflicts, there is a major conflict, the biggest conflict in your script.

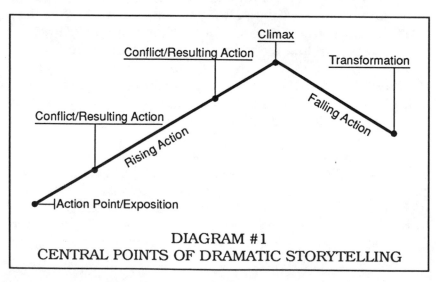

DIAGRAM #1
CENTRAL POINTS OF DRAMATIC STORYTELLING

CLIMAX

The major conflict is called a *climax* — the huge explosion in your work, a point where all boundaries crumble, and your hero/heroine must make a major decision from which there is no turning back. This is the major event that your protagonist must go through to reach his/her goal.

FALLING ACTION

The resulting action is short, one brief event. This might simply provide the audience with a sense of aftermath or it could tie up loose ends from a plot standpoint. It should provide a platform for the final stage — when your protagonist has an opportunity to show how he/she has grown through these experiences.

TRANSFORMATION

Your leading character is changed because of this series of conflict and action sequences; a goal has either been reached (comedy?) or discarded (tragedy?). There is resolution. Your character is forever changed because of the series of events he/she has experienced.

How do other characters fit into the traditional structure? The antagonist participates in the obstacles and usually the climax scene, and contributes to the escalation of the conflicts. The allies work with the protagonist to overcome the conflicts.

The antagonist may have a transformation, too, but it is more important that the protagonist's change be made clear. This can be shown through a final scene or event.

USE OF ONE-, TWO-, AND THREE-ACT STRUCTURES

In modern theater, most plays are written in the one- or two-act form. In a full-length two-act play, you repeat the diagram twice: You build to an Act One climax, and again to a larger Act Two climax. At the end of Act One, you provide a hook, a thread of unfinished action that can be used to start the action point of the second act (also, to make sure the audience comes back after intermission). Some full-length plays are 90-100 minutes without an intermission. These shows follow the diagram once, with more detail in each area than a short one-act.

In a one-act play, you use a condensed version of the diagram: immediate action point and exposition, fewer conflicts, climax, immediate transformation, end.

In film, it is varied a bit more: a three-act form with some changes in it, like an accordion. This three-act format is based on the older three-act stage play form. Act One is from pages 1-30. By the end of page thirty, an important circumstance must arise to propel your protagonist in the major action of the second act. Act Two is from pages 30-90. In Act Two, your hero/heroine must get into big trouble in pursuit of his/her goal. He/she must nearly give up, around page 75, but another big climax results that is overcome. Act Three is from pages 90-120, and is the resulting falling action from the Act Two Climax. Here, resolution is given.

In television, approximately each act follows the conflict/action sequence, with a hook at the end of acts, to propel the audience into the next act, after a commercial.

You can see how important an overall understanding and acceptance of the dramatic storytelling structure is; it is applied to every form of drama we have today.

VARIATIONS

Of course, not everyone follows this outline. Many variations of it exist. I enjoy experimenting myself; however, I'm not in favor of random, lazy choices. If you vary from this structure, you need to have a reason for doing so.

A popular theory now in effect is the Multi-Climactic Form (see Diagram #2). In this structure form, each conflict is worth the same dramatic weight as the initial scene. This has a ripple effect. There is not one big build to the climax; there is a scene with an equally important climax that follows each one. The scenes are related, but do not escalate. Some people see this as a cinematic effect, whether used in theater or film: scenes of approximately the same length, each with an equal conflict. Some argue that this is a more lifelike rhythm that audiences will relate to better.

Some writers do not give resolutions, preferring to leave a hanging, slice-of-life effect to a story; they feel this will allow the audience to draw their own conclusions.

I'm mentioning these examples to acknowledge that creativity knows no boundaries. If you wish to stray from the traditional path, just be sure that you have a very good reason for doing this. If you're working on your first dramatic script, I recommend sticking with the traditional.

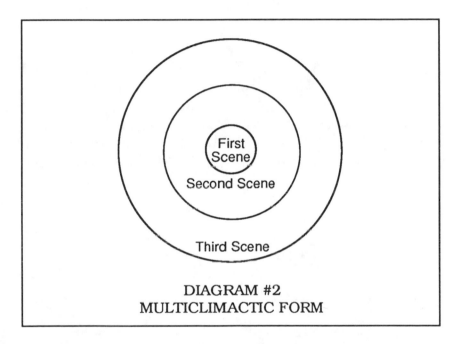

First Scene

Second Scene

Third Scene

DIAGRAM #2
MULTICLIMACTIC FORM

FLASHBACKS

A flashback is a jump backward in time, usually done to illuminate an aspect of character or to explain the foundation for a character's actions. This can be done in any dramatic medium, either for stage or screen. However, I would caution you to use this technique carefully. If action is really going forward, it is often frustrating to an audience to be put backward in time. I would urge you to try to show the same information through current character behavior. A flashback can be used as a crutch dramatically, and when poorly utilized, it will definitely lose an audience.

Many famous works, both literary and dramatic, use the flashback technique and use it brilliantly. Sometimes the piece will begin with narration that puts it immediately into flashback and then the rest of the story proceeds with forward action. Consider this: it's really a forward-moving story, with a hint of intrigue and tension from the word go. Make sure you can analyze how flashback functions in your script before you use it; don't let it slow your story down.

EXERCISES

1. Write a two-page outline of your script, using the key points from Diagram #1. Label each point; i.e., conflict, climax, etc.

2. Next, from your outline, write a five-page story version of your script, using present tense verbs ("Jane looks into the well and screams.") Try to make each paragraph represent a scene.

Now you have a rough outline and treatment for your script.

8.
Theme

The topic of theme is much maligned these days. Many authors will tell you not to worry about a theme — that they just started writing something and discovered what it was about as they went along. Or that they don't really have a point to get across. Or that they don't believe that authors should have anything in particular to say, etc., because art is what it is, and it's enough to create art for art's sake.

I've heard a lot of well-known authors say that they just let people get whatever they can out of their creations; they don't specify what their work is about beforehand.

That's great if you're a genius or extraordinarily lucky, but for those of us who don't want to bank on serendipity, attention to this element of craft will only heighten the caliber of the final product.

WHY HAVE A THEME?

I think life is too short not to have themes; for if there's no theme, if there's no important communication that you're trying to get across to an audience, then why go to the trouble to write in the first place? It takes effort to create a work of value; give it your best shot. If your work doesn't have a reason to reach an audience, it certainly won't sell.

Theme is the message or point you're trying to get across. It should not be confused with subject matter; that's the topic or general idea that you're writing about. Through use of theme you can express the point of view you have of life, the driving passion behind your exploration of something specific, something that has affected you and that you care about.

Think of yourself as a philosopher, using one of the most ancient forms of communication — drama — to get your point across. The real challenge is to entertain an audience while you explore a theme. It is my firm belief that all great dramatic works have these two elements in common: entertainment value and thematic passion.

It's easy to dismiss something when there is no real point to it. Sure, it's tempting to make people laugh for thirty to ninety minutes. But if they forget about what they saw as soon as it's over, you haven't really reached them on any important level.

As long as you're putting all this time into a project, why not have the highest aspirations? Why not try to achieve greatness? In terms of commerciality, works that make money do have strong themes — discernible motifs that people can relate to. That's one reason they're successful.

NAME THAT THEME

Clarity of theme focuses your work. You can use it as a constant tool as you're writing each section. I recommend writing down your theme on a piece of paper, and sticking it in a prominent place in your work area (i.e., above your computer screen or typewriter) so that you can refer to it as you write each scene.

In order to ensure that your work has a theme, it's important to specify what your theme is. At this time, you have a general idea of what you're writing about; go ahead and put it down in a simple sentence. Give the sentence three parts: a subject, an active verb, and an object (i.e. "heroism leads to glory"; "child abuse causes emotional damage"). The more active the verb is, the greater chance for action in your piece. But put it into a strong, sentence form.

The theme can change as you continue writing; you can make it more specific as you flesh out your story. But start by declaring your general theme as you know it, right now.

As you start to write scenes in our work in upcoming chapters, check to see that you continue to explore this theme on a moment-to-moment basis. No matter what happens in your scene, it should somehow resonate, amplify, clarify, or reflect your theme.

PROTAGONIST/MOTIF CONNECTION

Your protagonist's story is obviously directly connected to your theme. Whatever the plot is, the overall point is presented to the audience through your leading character's actions. Your motif is presented by what your protagonist does and thinks, and how your protagonist changes through a series of events. Whatever your protagonist does, especially at the end, will show the audience what your primary theme is. Allow your leading character to say a few lines of dialogue that directly express your theme; this is usually the best way to ensure that a motif is clear, and to give some excellent, profound dialogue to your central character.

EXERCISES

1. Theme Identification: Name your three favorite books. What are their storylines? Who are the stories about? What are their themes?

2. Theme Identification: Name your three favorite plays. Describe the plots of each. Who are the protagonists? What are their themes?

3. Theme Identification: What are the biggest film hits at this time? Describe what the films are about. Who are the important characters? What are their themes?

4. Analysis: Can you think of something you saw or read that frustrated you? Can you name its theme? Did it have too many themes?

9.
Dialogue

Let's review the developmental material currently in hand. You've got your character file, you've got your storyline developed in terms of major plot points, you've picked an appropriate setting, and you've got a theme prominently displayed somewhere in your writing area. You're getting close to the point where you can put your characters in motion and actually write the scenes of your project.

I've saved a discussion of dialogue until now because I have a specific point that I wanted to make about it. *Dialogue is not just talk.*

Commonly, beginning writers assume that dramatic writing is about talk (especially in the theater). I've seen first attempts at dramatic works that focus on clever twists of phrases but are totally unconnected to character and action.

This is a mistake. Dialogue comes from the mouths of your characters. But it is just one part of behavior, and behavior is connected to action. You define your characters by what they do. What they say is connected to the momentum of their deeds as well as to their hearts and minds.

In other words, make sure that there is an active motive behind what your characters say. Make them walk their talk. Everything they say is connected to an action or a feeling, something that propels them into motion.

Technically, dialogue comes from the Greek: *dia* means "two" and *logue* means "speech." Monologue means "one person's speech." So whenever you've got two or more people talking, you've got dialogue.

BE CHARACTER-SPECIFIC

Think of each character's speech as a fingerprint. What your character says is a microcosm of what he or she thinks, feels, and does. The entire background and future of your character can be disclosed in a few lines of dialogue. You can clearly depict psychological and physical states of your characters in one masterful stroke. But that's what makes it hard.

Your characters' speech must be directly linked to your characters; only they would say what they say. It should be so character-specific that, when reading it, after a few pages, we wouldn't need to see character names at all; we'd identify the speaker from the language, actions, and attitudes.

Especially be aware of making the characters go beyond the limitations of your own vocabulary and speech patterns. Look up new words; vary your own slang. Research the way people who live in your setting/arena talk. Learn the trade lexicon of the profession in which your character works.

CHARACTERISTICS OF DIALOGUE

Having a good ear and listening to people around you definitely helps you create dialogue that sounds real. There are a few characteristics of dialogue that are worth examining before writing words for your characters.

Incomplete Sentences

We rarely speak in complete sentences. Think about it. How often is your own speech interrupted by pauses, extra words, clauses that are incomplete, modifiers that dangle in the wind, and general stuttering? Sure, there are times when you can consciously use correct English, but aren't there other times when you don't? Compare the way you talk in a job interview to the way you chat with a close friend in confidence. There's a difference. Your characters' speech should reflect these same fluxes. Formal language is rare and should be used only in specific circumstances. Otherwise, expression occurs in fragments and clauses; some characters talk in a unique shorthand.

Lexicon

The vocabulary that your characters use should directly reflect their education level and life experiences. You can find out so much from the number of words in a character's normal lexicon. How often is slang used? How many polysyllabic words are employed? Are words used as weapons? Intimidation factors?

Musicality

Language has many melodic aspects to it, and well-written dialogue will, like music, sing. There are inflections, rhythms, cadences, intonations. See if you can feel the pulse in the rhythms of conversations around you. There is a definite beat. Each character should have his own beat, and the voices can be orchestrated in a scene — low parts, high parts, longer phrases, shorter phrases, all building to a crescendo at the climax of every scene.

Remember, dialogue is heard; it is received aurally. It is perceived not only through denotations but also through the sound. Be aware of this effect on the audience as well.

WRITTEN, NOT SPOKEN

Whenever you start writing dialogue, you should help establish an audience's belief in your character; you are asking them to suspend their skepticism of a fictional medium and accept this creation of yours as a real, breathing, thinking, living human being.

If your dialogue sounds like it's "written, not spoken," then the audience will notice the stiffness of your dialogue, notice that you haven't learned all the lessons of your craft, and be forced to acknowledge that this is a conceit, a piece of art. They will disinvest.

One way to ensure that your dialogue sounds "spoken" is to read it out loud, by yourself, either scene by scene or by ten-page increments.

If you have trouble with it, either from stumbling over words or in understanding the meaning of it, you can bet an audience will. Save yourself the anxiety of wondering how it sounds; read it yourself. See if it sounds like several people talking when you read it. If it all sounds the same, this is another potential problem area; like many instruments playing in an orchestra, you should be able to distinguish specific sounds as well as the symphony as a whole. In revision, change some rhythms and phrases to make the individual voices stronger.

TAPE

It's always good to tape record your initial readings of a scene. You can play it back and listen to it more objectively, with your eyes closed, really listening to see if the dialogue works. If you really want an adrenaline rush, you could try playing the tape for someone. There's something about the suggestion of audience that will allow you to hear the piece more "objectively," knowing that someone else will hear it. I highly recommend both of these methods to test out dialogue in the early phases of writing.

EXERCISES

1. FROM THE EAR TO THE PAGE. Be a spy. Tape record a conversation between three friends that lasts for thirty to sixty minutes. (Or tell them if you want; it won't really alter the exercise.) It can be about anything. Then transcribe the conversation; write it down on paper, identifying speakers' names and what they said, so it looks something like this in terms of formatting:

JILL

Why did you say that?

JACK

You know.

MARY

I want you to tell me.

JERRY

I wish you'd both shut up.

(Pause.)

After you've transcribed the entire thing, read it over. Is it a play? Why or why not? What do you learn about the natural flow of dialogue? Play your tape back as you read along with it. Examine the way the dialogue looks on the page and the way it plays when you aren't reading it. Note differences. Note length of sentences, interjections, variations in vocabulary.

2. PHRASES THAT INTEREST YOU. For one day, collect snatches of dialogue. Wherever you are, write down one phrase an hour that you hear and that strikes you as interesting. Maybe you do it on one sheet of paper; maybe several small pieces. At the end of the day, examine the collection. What stands out to you about these phrases? Was it the vocabulary, the denotation, or something else? Is character suggested through the phrases? Try to decide what was interesting about it when you heard it. Was it connected to action, character, or both?

3. MUSICAL ANALYSIS. Write down a few of your favorite expressions, things you've heard yourself say repeatedly. Write down enough to fill a couple of paragraphs. Now take a look at it. Count how many sentences/phrases you've written. How many average words per sentence? Do a syllable count: how many one-syllable, two-syllable, three-syllable, four-syllable words do you use? See how many stressed syllables there are in your sentences (the accented syllables, as pointed out in the dictionary or through scansion). Mark them. How could you characterize your own use of rhythm? Six beats per average sentence? More? Less? This is the same kind of analysis that you can do with your characters in order to emphasize the musicality of their speech. Every character should have a different pattern.

10.
Conflict & Action

In the simplest of terms, *conflict* is an emotional disturbance resulting from the collision of two opposing forces — a clash. *Action* is activity produced by energy in motion. This relationship — the clash and resulting motion of energy — is the essence of any dramatic scene. It is the recurring yet growing pattern of conflict and action that builds tension to the point of a final climax and resulting transformation.

Without this movement in a scene, nothing happens. There is absolute stagnation.

Think for a moment about how change occurs. Isn't it always through relationships of some kind: person-to-person, person-to-nature, person-to-society? You can't change in a vacuum. How do you know if you've changed until you have a way to demonstrate a different response through activities and interaction? How do you demonstrate something new unless there are ways to act out the new you?

Writers must find ways to show the audience the ever-evolving changes in their protagonists. In dramatic theory, there is no movement when there's no conflict/action escalation. The conflict/action progression has a sort of leap-frog effect, which produces tension as the stakes get higher in each instance (see Diagram #3, page 58). This is how to produce rising action.

STATIC ACTION

Static action occurs when there is no movement. People argue but nothing new happens; no higher level of understanding is reached. Their discussion is circular, and does not move the story forward. This can be a heated, passionate segment, but if no obstacle is removed or pursued, it's only a segment, a slice-of-life, and not a scene.

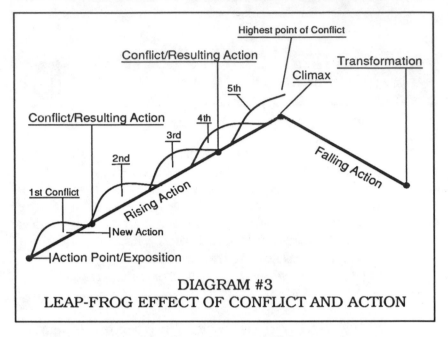

DIAGRAM #3
LEAP-FROG EFFECT OF CONFLICT AND ACTION

WRITING CONFLICT

What I've said above is the *theoretical* basis for conflict and action. Applying it is a bit harder. How do you start the actual writing process of this necessary dramatic dynamic?

Conflict begins with a desire on the part of your protagonist and an obstacle to that desire in the form of a problem. As your leading character attempts to achieve a goal, the obstacle in his or her way will produce a collision or clash that your protagonist must solve via action. Every action produces a reaction, a new climate, and consequently, the introduction of a new obstacle. This escalates as each new problem or obstacle is greater than the last, until finally, the biggest conflict of all occurs in the climax.

EVENTS AND ANTAGONISTS

The obstacles will occur through events and antagonists. This is where the idea of a three-dimensional antagonist will serve you well. An antagonist can orchestrate events to thwart your protagonist. In theater, there is often an understood, unseen antagonist, but in film, there is almost always a visible one.

In order to set up a direct protagonist/antagonist relationship, it's necessary to create an antagonist who wants the same thing your protagonist wants or whose desire to stop your antagonist fulfills his own specific needs. Remember, the more important and three-dimensional your "villain" is, the more impressive the conflict and resulting action.

This antagonist can be responsible for obstacles that your protagonist must go through in order to grow and finally achieve his or her goal, and inevitably, a transformation.

THEATER VERSUS FILM

In theater, because of the increasing pressure to keep casts to a minimum and because of the trends away from realism, as we mentioned earlier, there are fewer onstage antagonists these days. Often, the antagonist will be implied; obstacles are still there for your protagonist to go through, but not always shown via an antagonist.

In my play *Lady-Like*, about two Victorian "Ladies" who flee Ireland (with their maid) to start a female utopia in Wales, I restricted the cast size to three. I was able to show external conflicts (women versus society) without a direct antagonist. You saw their side of this conflict, but not the "perpetrators'" side. There is conflict in the play between the three women at different points, but no antagonist. They confront the problems of society, but no one character represents these problems.

In a film version of the same story, I would directly show the characters with whom they had conflicts: unhappy parents, disturbed siblings, aristocratic members of society, members of the British literati, etc. It would be presented "realistically"; however, the notion of conflict is present in both.

Below is an example of a scene from the play incorporating elements of conflict. The scene escalates; there is conflict between the characters as well as outside antagonism.

At this point in the play, the three women have been searching for a new home. They are running out of ideas, patience, and money. Lady Eleanor is the oldest (40's); Mary is the next oldest and their maid (30's). Sarah is in her early twenties. As the scene begins, they have been on their journey/escape from Ireland for nearly six months. They are homeless and trying to figure out where to settle.

                    SARAH
"Aberystyweth."

                    ELEANOR
Who wants to live near a seaport with all those
sailors?

                              (MARY starts to respond fa-
                              vorably then SARAH hands the
                              daybook to ELEANOR in an
                              abrupt manner. The trio
                              trudges on.)

                    MARY
"Machyinileth?"

                    SARAH
Too far from London.

                    ELEANOR
"Erbistock."

                    MARY
Disagreeably located for a dairy. Locked in a
valley.

                    SARAH
"Oswestry?"

                    ELEANOR
We said we'd live in Wales, not England.

                              (ELEANOR passes the daybook
                              back to SARAH. They trudge
                              on. Their hats are falling
                              off, their dresses are di-
                              sheveled. Annoyance is show-
                              ing in their faces and tones
                              of voice.)

                    MARY
"Denbigh?"

                    ___
                    60

ELEANOR (Sniffing)

Tawdry.

SARAH

"Llanwy...Llanwywreee....Llanwywreck?"

ELEANOR (Shrugging)

We can't pronounce it.

MARY

"Caernarvonshire?"

SARAH

The castle is too big.

ELEANOR (Blowing up)

Nothing pleases you.

SARAH

You're the one being disagreeable! We can't pronounce it, indeed! Nothing is good enough for your royal highness.

ELEANOR (Mimicking her)

"Too ancient."

SARAH

I don't want to reside in a cemetery quite yet, thank you. I do have a few years left of my youth and the hopes for some sort of life of quality.

ELEANOR

You're young. Go ahead, Miss Fair One! Not in the same boat with Mary and me, are you? At least you don't think so.

SARAH

I never said that. However, I could never be as pompous, as arrogant, as snitty as your ladyship. There you'll always win the contest.

                        ELEANOR
Why did I ever leave Ireland with you?

                        SARAH
Why did I ever write to you?

                        (They both cross away from
                        each other, with their arms
                        folded.)   .

                        SARAH
Flabby face!

                        ELEANOR
Impetuous child.   Grow up.

                        MARY
Oh, no.

                        (MARY sighs and rises.)

                        ELEANOR
Mary!

                        MARY
No.

                        ELEANOR
Now we've upset her as well.

                        SARAH
Who wouldn't be upset? We've had nothing for six
months but scenery and scrutiny.
                        (She throws the daybook
                        down.)

                        ELEANOR
The hats weren't my idea.

                        SARAH
I'd like my annuity back. This clearly isn't working out.

ELEANOR

Your annuity is gone. Ask Mary. We've barely
fifty pounds left.

SARAH (Sarcastically)

You've done an admirable job with the finances.

ELEANOR

We're getting by.

SARAH

You call this getting by?

ELEANOR

We're still alive. That's success in the wilds of
this country. I've done the best I could. You
hardly know how to take care of yourself.

SARAH

I'd like to go back to Ireland. Give me whatever
it takes. I don't care how much you have left.

ELEANOR

Always thinking of your own needs. How are Mary
and I to get by?

SARAH

I'll take Mary back with me.

ELEANOR

What if she doesn't want to leave?

SARAH

Then the two of you can fend for yourselves in this
god-forsaken forest. Wherever we are.

ELEANOR

You're vile.

SARAH

You're impossible.

ELEANOR

You're irrational.

SARAH

You never cared about me. You used me for my money—to get yourself out of dire straits. Maybe my uncle was right after all.

ELEANOR

You don't know what love is, or goodness, or kindness, or any matter of the heart!

SARAH

How am I supposed to know? I've never had any before.

> (Suddenly, stones hit the ground near their feet—first a few, then a few more. A commotion is heard.)

SARAH

What's this?

ELEANOR

They want to kill us. (To throwers) Stop. Stop. We'll move along.

SARAH

They think we're witches or something. We're not witches. We're Catholics.

ELEANOR

Sarah! (Pulls her into a run.) They'll burn us at a stake! Run!

> (The stones stop. ELEANOR grabs SARAH and they hurry away.)

ELEANOR

We can't fight in public. It attracts too much attention from the barbarians.

SARAH

Who can blame them? Weird spinsters yelling in the streets. This gets better and better. We've no place to live, eat, fight—let alone love. This is hopeless.

(MARY enters.)

MARY

See that cottage way up on the hill. A few miles away. The brown one.

SARAH

It's alone?

MARY

Yes. And it's ours, for twenty pounds a year.

(ELEANOR crosses to get a better view of it.)

ELEANOR

Where are we now, Mary?

MARY

Llangollen, mum. It's a very pretty place. There's a river nearby. The Dee. And way to the east, see those remains? They call it Crow Castle. Very mysterious. (She points.) And over to the south, a hill to climb, the Dinas Bran.

SARAH (Sullenly)

It's a regular mountain.

MARY

They say anybody can live here for a song, for nothing, so cheap it is.

ELEANOR

It's quite lovely.

SARAH

We're so poor that if it has a roof and a door
you'd call it charming.

MARY

The town itself isn't much. A tavern, a shop or
two. By the way, did I ever tell you that I used
to run a tavern? In the West?

ELEANOR

No. You never did.

MARY

Well, we'll see how this one's doing. Listen,
there's also a waterfall. Can you hear it?

(They pause listening.)

SARAH

I hope it drowns out the sound of my tears.

ELEANOR

Do we have twenty pounds?

MARY

Just barely.

ELEANOR

Then let's take a look at the place.

TENSION

If each scene is more important than the scene before, in terms
of heightened stakes for the protagonist, tension automatically
builds. If there is no forward movement, in terms of conflict/
resulting action, then there will be no tension. Tension is
almost a by-product of escalation.

Tension helps hold an audience's interest, through the stress caused in the emotional stakes of your protagonist and the story. In other words, the audience cares about what happens; they have an emotional investment in the outcome of your story.

Moving your story along through these connected sequences, with ever-growing stakes, will provide your audience with an emotional pay-off in the climax and produce tension as you tell your tale.

EXERCISES

1. CONFLICT: Think of an object, a physical object, something that two different people could want. Make up the two people, and write a fight for that object. Make sure one of the people wins. Who wins? Why? Where is the turning point of the fight?

2. STATICITY: Rewrite that scene without either person wanting the object. Compare the differences in the scenes.

3. ACTION: Imagine two inanimate objects; pick something out from the room that you're currently in (i.e., a light bulb and a trash can). Write a scene between these two objects, about doing something. Is there any action? Or is it just clever dialogue?

11.
Technical Elements, Voice, & Unity

This chapter is about physical elements (the things you should know about how your work will be mounted and presented), voice (the unique way you write), and unity (the way all things come together). These are some final important elements to add to your study of dramatic writing.

TECHNICAL ELEMENTS

You should be aware of the technical requirements of any medium that you are writing in, be it for stage or screen. Technical considerations are more complex for the screen, because of all the elements I'm going to describe below and how they work for the camera. (If you are writing a screenplay or teleplay, I urge you to do additional research on your own to develop further expertise on the subject.)

When I first began to write for the stage, I spent a lot more time thinking about actors and dialogue than how the lights work and who was going to design costumes. I saw shows that were dazzling from a technical standpoint, but because I didn't have the slightest idea how some of the things were done, I decided such spectacles would be out of my creative realm as a writer.

As luck would have it, I ended up having to do some backstage work in the early 1980s, and got to know designers and production staff responsible for mounting some complicated shows. This influence began to show in my work; other playwrights asked me how I had come up with such physical, creative ideas — it really made some of my work stand out because it seemed "theatrical" and visual. Designers and directors also commented on these elements; I even got a couple of productions by request of designers who wanted to design some of these "theatrical" creations.

The change came in my work when I developed a respect and knowledge of technical elements and how they work. I quit thinking it wasn't a writer's domain; I embraced it as an important way to create in the dramatic form. Get familiar with this part of production.

I'm going to detail some of the technical elements involved in stage presentation. These are less complicated than for the screen but involve some of the same basic principles, and will help you, as a writer, to visualize and create in a three-dimensional medium.

Lighting

An audience won't be able to see anything without proper light on the subject. A lighting designer will be responsible for creating the lighting to showcase your actors, the set, and the playing area.

Keep in mind the number of *areas* that you use onstage. Are you using the entire stage or parts of it, at different points with quick transitions? These will be challenges for designers; as a rule, it's best to keep the number of areas used to a minimum.

Be aware of the fact that if you're working in a small theater (most of us start out that way), the lighting capabilities in each venue may vary — from real instruments to tin cans. This can make highly complicated lighting requirements a real problem. Make sure that you've thought the cues through and that you've given the most basic descriptions of lights — whatever is necessary to show the time of day and/or mood of your work.

If you want to show passage of time, indicate lighting *fades* (i.e., write LIGHTS FADE at the end of a scene). If you want to show different locations, indicate lighting *crossfades* (where the lights shift quickly from one side of the stage to the other, i.e., LIGHTS CROSSFADE FROM SR TO CENTER).

Sound

It often amazes me how much can be suggested through sound and lights. Sound can indicate locale (ocean waves can establish a sea coast; traffic noises can establish an urban setting), time of day (birds chirping evoke dawn/sunrise), moods (danger can be underscored through certain sounds), weather (a thunderstorm or high wind). Think about how sound could enhance your work and write in descriptive cues to promote the environmental aspects of your scene.

Props

Objects that are used by your characters can help define them and provide action — things they hold and use. Specify props that are interesting and character-specific. As always, if you can reduce the number of props required, it makes the play less expensive to produce. That's why whatever props used are so important; props make a visual impact.

Props can also show what is important to your characters — their values can be illustrated through what they own and how they take care of their belongings. A classic example of this is the way the character of Laura in Tennessee Williams' play, *The Glass Menagerie*, handles her collection of glass animals. Because she keeps them polished and on display, and delves into periods of fantasy about them, the audience knows quite a few things about her without having to be told: she is out of touch with the real world; she's more at ease dealing with inanimate things than humans. Her affinity for the unicorn — her favorite piece that is damaged in the scene with the gentleman caller — further defines her character. Her limp, a physical handicap, is verbally and visually compared to the unicorn's horn; without this disability, she's afraid there's nothing unique about her. When the unicorn's horn is accidentally broken, and Laura sadly holds it in the light, we see the correlation between character and prop: it has become metaphor.

Again, this is a powerful three-dimensional way to communicate to your audience.

Sets

We discussed setting in detail in Chapter 6. The set is what is built to simulate the environment; it can look realistic or just be suggestive of realism. It may be abstract or it may be whatever you feel would serve the tone of your piece. Take care to describe it. Remember that the fewer locales you have, the better in terms of production cost.

Try to visualize how the set will look. If you have any suggestions, even though the set will be designed by a professional, write in what you envision. The playwright's purview is the initial one. Most designers like to know what the play-wright, in their heart of hearts, would like to see up there. Even though they may not use it, it is helpful to designers/directors/producers to have an initial image, a springboard, to start with.

Costumes

Clothes make the man; are we what we wear? Well, at least for a certain event at a specific point in time. Take time to think about what your characters' apparel says about them. The number of costume changes should be kept to a minimum due to expenses, but variety is always more interesting to an audience.

Costumes are part of the visual spectacle, a major part. A designer will ultimately be responsible for the creative input needed to clothe the cast, but any ideas from you will only help your work breathe from the page . . . to the stage . . .

Technical Summary

Of course, the entire physical process will be overseen by a director, but don't let anyone tell you not to worry about the physical details. The genesis of the project is with the writer. Ask for what you want; be as creative as possible with the three-dimensional aspects of this art. As we noted in the beginning, this is one reason the dramatic form is unique. Use technical aspects to your advantage.

VOICE

You are writing something that is unique; *you* are writing it, at this point in time, with a specific perspective on the world and life. This has never happened before. Is there any way your work cannot therefore be unique?

Get specific about what makes your writing and your ideas different from other things you know. Tap into the strength of *voice*.

Developing Voice

It may sound here as though we're talking about singers. Voice is related to music. The way a singer interprets a song and hits the notes is what makes a real "voice." The same is true for a writer. There are specific characteristics of your writing, related to your use of dramatic principles, that only you have.

These characteristics may be your use of imagery, your use of metaphors, the regional flavor of your dialogue, the power of your theme, or a combination of all of the above (or none of the above — something else!). Whatever is unique about your style and view is what is called "voice."

Imagine you're in a large kitchen, full of creative chefs. Each of you has the same ten ingredients to work with — laid out in front of you on a counter. But you're going to dream up your own individual recipes — make something new and do it your own way. When the cooking is done, there will be a smorgasbord; the group will not have made the same things. Your final product and how it's different from the others will say a lot about your voice.

Think about who your favorite writers are. What is it that attracts you to their work? I've often admired the heart and lyricism in Tennessee Williams' work; the political perspectives in Caryll Churchill's work; the zany humor in Christopher Durang's work, Milcha Sanchez-Scott's use of symbol, metaphor, and setting; and the political satire of George C. Wolfe, to name a few. These writers say things in a way no one else can.

Writers pride themselves on these points of creative individualism. If we were to take a room full of twenty writers and give them all the same topic . . . say, something about conflict on Wall Street . . . we'd get twenty different interpretations of even so vague an idea. Voice is one important reason this would occur. We each express ourselves from our own frame of reference, unique to us. It's the way we see the world, the reasons we think the way we do, seeing the world right now.

Celebrate what makes your writing different but don't use it as a mask to cover what doesn't work. Intuitively, you know what things in your work so far are coming together. Pat yourself on the back. Count these as strengths. But always strive to improve areas of weakness.

UNITY OF ELEMENTS

All the elements we've discussed in terms of principles of your craft should work together as a whole to bring your work to life. All craft elements should coalesce: character, setting, story, theme, dialogue, conflict/action, technical elements, and voice. If one element stands out above the others, if it's clear that your plot is more interesting than your characters, for instance, then there is a breakdown of unity.

The craft of dramatic writing works because all these elements are part of a creative, life-giving process that you've deliberately put together in order to give birth to your ideas in a three-dimensional way. Each has a specific function but they work together, like a team. Every principle should pull its own weight.

The combined effort should illustrate your theme and entertain; the principles are vessels for your ideas. Make sure you control these tools and are clear on how they serve you in regards to your project. Otherwise, they might be controlling you.

EXERCISES

Technical Elements

1. SET DESCRIPTION: Describe a set for a script you'd like to write. Write several paragraphs using details; specifically use stage directions (stage right, stage center, stage left, etc.).

2. PROPS: Write a two-line description of each of the following: your protagonist's favorite comb, your protagonist's pillow, a secondary character's gun, a secondary character's briefcase.

3. COSTUMES: Describe your protagonist's favorite dress apparel. Describe your protagonist's most comfortable clothing.

4. SOUND AND LIGHTS: Write a sound and lighting description for the beginning of your project. Evoke mood, time, weather, activity, and locale.

Voice

1. Evaluate your strengths as a writer. What qualities do you have that make you different?

2. What unique view can you give an audience that will make them remember your work?

3. Who are your favorite writers? Do they have distinct "voices"?

Unity

4. UNITY OF ALL ELEMENTS. Are all the major elements of your work in place: character, story, setting, theme, dialogue, conflict, action, technical elements, and voice? Write a brief outline that defines all these elements in your project. This sheet can serve as another guide; as you begin your scene-writing process, you may refer to this sheet as well to ensure you stay on track with your writing goals.

12.
Writing Scenes
& Acts

Now you're ready to start writing your dramatic writing project. You've had a long gestation period of planning and organizing. Your creative juices have been stimulated. (If they haven't been, go back and do the exercises in the preceding chapters.) I'm sure you've gotten the impression that I feel your best writing will be ensured by a pre-writing period that solves many of your structural problems before you start. And you also know that the only real way to learn how to write is to do it, through study and exercises, trial and error.

BUILDING A SCENE

Now you can be spontaneous; you've done the initial part, the difficult part. You have done the conscious planning. Now you can explore, be loose and free.

You can write your first scene.

What exactly is a scene? A unit of action, where something happens, usually in *beats*, which are even smaller units of action and new thoughts. Let me reiterate: Something happens. There's action. At the end of the scene, there is a new condition that has been set up through the action that occurred in the scene. It can be long or short; there's no hard rule for this in the theater, although for the screen most scenes are three to five pages long.

I recommend that you use the standard playwriting format as shown below for these initial scene attempts.

```
                    ELEANOR
Our purpose in retirement is fourfold.  One, we come here
never to leave until death do us part.  Two, we shall
devote hearts and minds to self-improvement.  Three, we
eschew the vanity of society.  And four, we plan to
beautify our surroundings.
```

SARAH

Five, we'll better the lot of the poor when possible.

ELEANOR

We are the poor.

SARAH

Then the other poor when possible.

ELEANOR

Fine. Here's to Plas Newydd.

> (ELEANOR breaks the bottle on
> the side of the house. Noth-
> ing comes out.)

MARY

Here, here.

SARAH

It's empty.

ELEANOR

Not to waste any of the good stuff. Maestro, music
please!

> (MARY starts to hum and mo-
> tions for ELEANOR and SARAH
> to dance. They take a spin
> around the garden, waltzing.
> SARAH is stiff at first but
> slowly loosens up. Soon,
> ELEANOR and SARAH join MARY
> in humming.)

ELEANOR

La la la la la la---

SARAH

La la la la la la---

> (As ELEANOR and SARAH carry
> the melody, MARY exits.
> Soon, ELEANOR and SARAH sit
> on a garden bench.)

ELEANOR
Look around you. In a few months we have turned this
place into a veritable paradise.

Excerpt from LADY-LIKE
Copyright © 1990 by Laura Shamas

Before you do a first draft, if you're writing a screenplay or teleplay, look up the format in Chapters 20 and 21. Put the characters' names in capital letters in the center of the page, when they are speaking, with the dialogue immediately under it, single-spaced. Skip two spaces in between speakers. Descriptions of action on stage should run from the center of the page to the right margin, and be placed in parentheses. Put the names of characters in all capital letters when mentioned in stage directions. In order to get the hang of the margins, try typing the sample page once, to get the feel for the correct placement from a technical standpoint.

Okay, enough procrastination. That's the superficial stuff you need to know to start. But how are you going to write a scene?

Just do it.

Go back to our numerous plot outlines, and our discussion of conflict and action. Take a deep breath. And do it.

What action point did you pick? Start there. Limit your initial try to three to five pages. Rev up your favorite writing utensil — pencil, fountain pen, typewriter, personal computer — and go for it. It doesn't matter if it takes you five minutes or five hours; have fun with it. Don't labor over single sentences — save that for the rewriting phase. See how quickly you can get the initial seed of your idea down on paper, and try not to judge the material as you create it.

Writers do themselves great harm by judging their work prematurely. Some people experience an initial sinking feeling about every line; they feel it warrants immediate revision, and it isn't worth it to continue if it all doesn't "sing." Nonsense. You're going to have to rewrite eventually, for some reason or another, so just know you'll have some time to make it perfect later. It's much easier to work on revision than to stare at a blank page. *Write.*

Stop here and write. It's worth it. This is why you bought the book, isn't it?

After writing your scene, read it out loud. Tape record it. How does it sound? Does it build to an arc/climax? Is there conflict? Is there action? Do you have a sense of character? Is the setting established? Is there an obstacle? Does the dialogue sound real? Is the dialogue character-specific? Do you love it?

If you've answered yes to all these questions, you may have a "writer's high," similar to a "runner's high." There is a euphoria that comes with any creative act, especially after finishing it. In fact, studies on effective writers' habits show that procrastination is a common thread among productive writers, and a feeling of accomplishment afterwards pervades as well. Congratulations.

If you don't feel euphoric, you may have that other common response, "writer's high anxiety." It's when you have both of these responses at the same time that it can get really confusing! It's amazing how easy it is to grow accustomed to both the high and the anxiety; writers cope somehow.

BUILDING AN ACT

Well, you've officially begun the actual writing process. The thought of putting together an entire act may seem mind-boggling to you, but it's really a methodical repetition, and escalation, of the same principles you just put to use in your first scene. Putting a full unit together involves increasing the stakes with each scene — the creation of a path filled with conflict and action that can be approached in segments; you write it in chunks. Remember that there is a big moment of climax at the end of the act and a planted "hook," a seed of conflict to kick off the second act with an "action point."

In plays, acts average forty-five to fifty-five pages; in screenplays, first and third acts are around thirty pages each, and the second act expands to around sixty pages. With teleplays, there is variation; each act is around twelve minutes of material.

Ready to continue?

EXERCISES

1. Complete an outline of all your scenes, based on your story, which you wrote out in detail in previous chapters. Incorporate all characters.

2. Write a paragraph on each scene. Describe what the action is in each — the essence of what is going on.

You now have a formal outline of your script.

13.
Writing the
First Draft

This is the chapter where I start to sound like a cheerleader. You can do it. Take that outline and start plowing through it. Write a scene a day — more if you can. You've got your maps: it's time to sail.

Remember when we discussed the idea of commitment? Now's the time to show how responsible you are. You made commitment to this idea and now, as you bring it to life, you're going to learn to live with it. It really needs you right now; it's just this baby of an idea, floundering around, crying out for love and attention. If you don't nurture it every day, form it on a disciplined basis, how will it survive?

It won't. Your project will lose all connection with you. You started this. You've got a responsibility to the idea and to yourself — to your talent and desire to write — to finish what you started.

Personally, I always dread writing the first draft — that is, until I start it. Once I start, I cannot stop. It completely enthralls me; several of my plays, including the one that is most successful to date, had first drafts that were completed in one weekend. Now that's not to say that they didn't go through countless revisions. Believe me, they did — for years! But it is a sign of how engrossing and enthralling the process of writing is, once you get into it. Even though the thought can be overwhelming, like many things in life, after you take the plunge, you can't imagine why you ever hesitated.

When you play an instrument, you must practice every day. If you're an athlete, you must work out on a regular basis. The same thing is true of your mental muscles — which are used in writing — as well as your creative juices. You *must* try them out every day.

The project becomes less imposing the further along you get. Take several baby steps and then see how far you've come. You have the list of scenes, an outline. You can methodically cross them out as you go along. Or, because of your excellent pre-planning, you can even skip around and do a scene out of sequence, if you've got a case of (heaven forbid!) writer's block. But the important thing is to write, write, write. You're not getting any younger. You've got all the tools in front of you, and you've got this book.

I'm pulling for you.

Think of the satisfaction you'll have when you can hold an entire first act in your hand . . . a second act . . . maybe even a third. Think of how much fun it will be to copy and photocopy this manuscript, and buy a binder for it. (Well, maybe office supplies don't excite you that much yet. Keep writing. They will.)

INCENTIVE — AN AUDIENCE

Remember that audience we discussed? Now's the time to visualize them. Be specific about them if you want to: imagine your mate, brother, sister, mother, father, best friend, boss, etc., reading this brilliant manuscript that you've just completed. Doesn't that make you want to get right to your story?

INCENTIVE — OTHER PRODUCED WORK

Go see a bad play or film and see how much it makes you want to create something new, refreshing, that has your own unique point of view in it. A little competitive edge is healthy. If you are deeply committed to writing, you should appreciate the talents of others but desire to make your own contribution as well. A little sniff of the current marketplace usually does get the blood circulating in the typing fingers.

INCENTIVE — FOR YOU

You have something you need or want to express. You may have been wanting to do this for a long time, or just by chance, you picked up this book. Whatever has led you to this point will yield the same results: you have an interest in dramatic writing. You may be trying to sort through personal events from the past, or explore a new area of life, find out about something that fascinates you. Whatever the reason, complete the task and see what you get out of it. Maybe you'll find you want to be a writer. Maybe you'll find you have a new and profound respect for those who do write for a living. Maybe it will become an occasional hobby. Maybe it will solve a problem. But you owe it to yourself to find out what your specific attraction to it will yield. Finish the draft for *yourself.*

INCENTIVE — REWARD

Find ways to reward yourself as you finish each scene or segment. Celebrate as you go along. Writing in the dramatic form is worthy of a few champagne moments upon completion of pages. Give yourself delicious rewards after each major segment. These can be culinary, physical, spiritual — whatever works for you. Give yourself things to look forward to — lunch breaks with friends after two hours of work, or a game of tennis when you finish your first act. Make the process a fun one.

INCENTIVE — THE SOONER YOU FINISH, THE SOONER YOU CAN SHOP IT AROUND

Let's be practical. The more quickly you get this project under your belt, the sooner you can explore other aspects of reward: productions, options, etc. The process of marketing is a long one; finish your draft so you can get to see your piece on its feet or start to sell it.

INCENTIVE — OTHER PEOPLE HAVE FINISHED THEM

If the process of dramatic writing is really so hard, why have so many other people done it? If they did it, so can you. (This argument only works for me when I'm really tired, so I put it here near the end of this chapter, in case you were feeling a bit fatigued, too.) Join the legions of people who have completed a play or screenplay or teleplay. It's a fun group.

INCENTIVE — YOU LOVE THE MEDIUM

You love dramatic writing so much that you simply must make a contribution to this medium. You've got theater in your blood. You've got films on the brain. You've got TV in your bones. These are in the essence of your soul. You're planning to move the medium forward with your originality. We need new geniuses. Go for it.

INCENTIVE — IT'S AN ASSIGNMENT

You're in a class and you've got to do this for a grade. You need to pass this class. Need I say more?

INCENTIVE — COURAGE

This is one of the bravest things you've ever done, so it will show how courageous you are if you get it down. What a strength of character — to say you want to complete an artistic task, learn how it's done, and actually do it! Pouring your thoughts out to strangers is scary but if you finish, you'll have the pages in your hands and the courage to show your draft to others; the hardest part will be behind you.

EXERCISE

Write your first draft.

14.
Writer's Block

"Writer's Block." The dreaded term. Seeing it in print is enough to make any scribe tremble. It means you write to a certain point and then, lo and behold, you can write no more, no matter how hard you try. There is scientific evidence that it exists. However, don't let that make it sound attractive (I know, you're like me; you'll use any excuse to stop writing). It's easy to get discouraged; other people in the real world will try to dissuade you, so don't slow yourself down! Don't psyche yourself out. Don't be destructive. If you feel "blocked," use the exercises at the end of the chapter to help you get over it.

We live in a world of stress. There is more tension than ever before: more responsibilities on the job, complex family situations, less clean air to breathe, new technological developments to contend with. If you are trying to live "the writing life," it means you probably have twice as many stress factors as other people: you may have a full-time job in addition to your foray into writing. You may stare at a computer screen night and day, due to work and writing pressures. You may not exercise enough or sleep well. You may be a wreck — a creative genius but a wreck.

Of course you'll feel "blocked" at times. I feel blocked just contemplating our lifestyle. But don't let that stop you from writing. Go ahead and feel blocked for a while and then get back to work.

It's possible your brain can get tired. It's hard to be profound all the time. Writing is so creative, so mental. Sometimes you need to get up and run around, or look at the sun or the moon or the stars to remind you that there's a world other than the one you're so diligently trying to create on the page.

It can be a relief to stop working! You may really want to eat or sleep so you think, "This stuff is awful. I can't write another word. Maybe it'll be better tomorrow." If you really go back to it and start writing tomorrow, then just call that a long break and not "Writer's Block."

True "Writer's Block" means you try to write the next day, and you clean your desk instead. Or you put it off for another day and count ants walking on the sidewalk for an afternoon during your scheduled writing time. Or a week later, writing another sentence seems like an impossibility. Or in a month, when you reread it, you have no idea why you started the project and wonder who really wrote the darn thing.

If you are truly blocked, it may be a sign that you've hit upon a writing problem that you can't quite overcome. Sure, it may be a sign that there's a structural problem, or a reconsideration necessary for some important part of your story.

If that's the case, it's really easy to solve. All you need to do is think clearly and swiftly. Reread what you've got and then as quickly as possible, in 60 to 120 seconds if you can, jot down some rough ideas about where the piece is going (not where you'd planned it to go, but where you instinctively feel it's going). This may be the answer; you may need to change direction. Go with what interests you. If you find your story significantly changed, you can start over or keep going in the new direction. Either way, you're on the road to discovery and no longer blocked.

DON'T GIVE UP

You learn little from abandoning a project due to "Writer's Block." Writing is rewriting. You'll learn so much more from finishing something, viewing it in its entirety, and thinking about its merits from an objective standpoint than completely throwing something away. What a waste! You've done enough forethought; you shouldn't be writing yourself into a corner. You chose that path for some reason. It attracted you on some level — a level important enough for you to commit to it. Honor that commitment. You made a contract with yourself. You'd want others to honor their commitments to you. Show yourself the same integrity.

Sometimes, feeling blocked is a great sign. It can show that your project is about something that means a lot to you — you might be learning something about yourself or the world or the future or the collective unconscious. It can be scary to face the truth. Writing from the heart is an act of bravery. The things that are the toughest for us to write may turn out to be the most meaningful. Rise to the challenge; seek catharsis. Keep going.

If I may be completely honest with you, as I mentioned in Chapter 12, studies show that some degree of procrastination is completely normal and even a habit of effective writers. You can play hooky sometimes and feel you're in good company.

But writing is a serious business. You're building new worlds; you're exploring your own mind; you're offering ideas and feelings for others to embrace or connect with; come back refreshed but come back. Don't neglect that world you're constructing; it's important. It's delicate. You're the only one who can do it. In your way.

Somewhere, maybe not so far from where you live right now, maybe not so far from where you're sitting as you read this, there's a writer, a writer whose pen is gushing like a fountain. This writer can't type quickly enough; the words flow like a river. This writer is laughing from the sheer ecstasy of writing, high on creativity. This writer can't remember when it's lunchtime or suppertime. This writer looks at a clock and is surprised to learn that it's 2:00 A.M. This writer's computer has been on for eight hours. This writer doesn't care what day it is — except in the script that's in process. This writer doesn't return phone calls for a few days. This writer writes.

This could be you.

EXERCISES

1. A WEEK OF FIFTEEN-MINUTE SESSIONS. Are you truly having problems writing? Try the short-term approach. Take only fifteen minutes a day, maybe during your lunch hour, or right when you wake up, before your household gets too busy. It should be fifteen minutes of guaranteed peace. And write as fast as you can, following your outline/scenes. Time yourself. Only write for fifteen minutes. Don't think or analyze. Just write. And then put it away after fifteen minutes. Don't reread it. The next day, do the same thing at the same time, in the same way, continuing from where you stopped. At the end of the week, even if you have only seven pages, you will have finished your scene! Read the whole thing. Revise it. The following week, lengthen your writing sessions to twenty-five minutes, until your flow is back. This approach also strengthens a disciplined commitment to writing every day. This exercise was inspired by Dorothea Brande's book, *Becoming A Writer*, which has excellent guidelines for overcoming self-criticism during the writing process and other spiritual approaches to creativity. I highly recommend it. (See "Recommended Reading" in the Appendix for more details.)

2. A DAY OF WRITING — NO EXIT. This is for the hard-core "get me over this block business quickly" people. You know you've got some writing to do. Put aside six hours to write, all at once, for one day. Make sure *no one can reach you.* Have some food around. Make sure there are plenty of office supplies at your disposal (plenty of paper!); in other words, NO WAY OUT.

Sit down. Place a clock nearby. Don't try to plan what you're going to write, especially if you've been blocked. Just sit down and start to write. Write anything. Write nonsensical sentences. But write. The first hour write anything. This will be the hardest hour. Don't doodle; write sentences. The second hour, keep writing, anything. About this time, believe me, you'll start to have an idea. The third hour, write what your heart feels. Keep writing. The fourth hour will have a slight lull, but should be infinitely more inspired than the first hour. By the last hour, what you're writing should be gold, I promise. You'll be cooking. Maybe you'll have come back around to your project; maybe this will be a whole new project or a new approach to your initial idea. But you'll have a lot written and you'll have gotten over "Writer's Block."

15.
Criticism as
 Your Ally

You've completed the first draft. Now you need to put it away for a few days.

You've lost all objectivity about the work, anyway; you need to gain some fresh perspectives. Don't think about your project for awhile — not for a really long time, a week at most, but long enough for you to look at the pages and not know what's coming next. Get unfamiliar with it.

Then, take a quiet afternoon and grab something to drink. Pick up your script and read it with virginal eyes. Peruse it in this objective state and take notes on how you think it's working.

You've begun the process of gathering information about how your script works. This is the first step in a long process of passing your work around to others in order to get "objective" feedback. There are three different stages: the One-on-One Stage, the Cold Reading Stage, and the Workshop Level. You will probably want to revise after every stage of the process; it will be hard to know what to listen to. But that's the reason you must embrace criticism as your ally. Don't be defensive. Listen to what people have to say; you're able to do that because you want to know how effective your work is. Ultimately, this feedback will make your script (and you) stronger. You will know what works. You will be able to improve what doesn't work. What could be more beneficial than that?

CRITICISM

Everyone has an opinion and you're going to be bombarded with a ton of ideas, most of them conflicting, most of them from people you shouldn't listen to anyway. Some of it can even make you angry, depending on how it's delivered. That's why your initial reaction to the draft, in your objective state, is so important. Your notes on rereading your work are crucial guidelines; they will establish a framework off which you can bounce all other criticism. Your notes will delineate things about your script that you honestly feel work or don't work. Other people can confirm or refute your instincts, but remember, it's *your* work. Your name is on it, so you are the final judge of what's going to make it better. Never discount the intuitive feelings you have about your work. As the creator, you will have the strongest ties to it. Trust your instincts.

TAKING NOTES

When you start to pass your script around, let's say to the first five people you ask to read it, it's a good idea to write down their reaction to your work; take notes on what they say. Hearing other people's opinions is the first step towards reaching an audience; in fact, the initial readers of your work are your audience — the first new eyes to take in what you've created.

You really only will incorporate a small amount of the suggestions that you receive, but it's important to hear several different opinions after you've finished the first draft.

Take notes while you listen; doing so gives you something active to do while you're listening to what's said. Writing while you listen may also help defuse any extreme reactions to their comments — you have to write it down rather than react to it. Additionally, you can transcribe their comments in ways that make sense to you and are pertinent to your script; you can write in your own code or shorthand. Obviously, these sheets become references for you to use during your revision drafts, so it's good to keep them around.

Another good thing to do is to tape record critique sessions. I still recommend copying down notes while you tape record. There's a powerless feeling that comes while listening to litanies of things that need to be fixed, even when the information is delivered in the kindest way possible. If you're actively interpreting it, it will be more meaningful to you, and it will underscore the fact that you are gathering information; you are trying to reach some sort of consensus about your creative work.

ONE-ON-ONE

Who should you give your work to, at the earliest stage? Someone you trust. It's asking a lot of people to read your work and give you feedback. You're taking their time. You're putting them on the spot. They are really doing you a favor. Make sure it's someone who (a) wants to do it, (b) has some background, expertise, and/or intelligence that pertains to the process, and (c) will be honest with you. If the reader will not really tell you what he or she thinks, you're wasting his/her time and yours.

In other words, be careful and selective with this initial distribution of the first draft. You might not want to show it at all. But this is why you wrote it. You've got to give it over or it will never be "presented"; that's one of the requirements of the dramatic form — others participate in bringing it to life. But don't give it to everyone who expresses an interest (or to people who don't, for that matter). Use discretion. Pick out five people whose opinions you'd like to hear. After they've read it, ask to meet with them, promising not to take up too much of their time. Assure them that you want to listen to their feedback.

No one wants to be trapped with a first-time writer who is overly defensive. A word about defensiveness: it never helps you. You need to listen to what people are saying. If you are really being attacked so heavily that your personal integrity is threatened, get up and leave the room, but leave your tape recorder running. Don't start an argument. I really encourage new writers to close their mouths in critique sessions; let your work speak for you.

I know how hard this can be. In the 1980s, I sat through many public critique sessions connected to readings and workshop performances of my plays. After the first one, which seemed interminable, I wanted to burn the entire script; in fact, a good friend of mine who is now a director had to stop me. That initial play was published a year and a half later, but I spent a great deal of time in the following months agonizing over what was said in that critique session and taking it personally, when I could have been revising the play in a professional manner! Don't make the same mistake I did.

My father, who is a successful businessman, really helped me realize that you present a public image, as a living writer, taking criticism during discussions; if you're overly cranky, it's not a great calling card for future work. He told me, after one particularly harrowing session, to look at it as a marketing opportunity and not as an ordeal. After acknowledging the public relations potential of these sessions, I wrote a few notes down on my notepad before the sessions began. "Smile, write something down, and look up" was one thing I wrote on the pad, so that whenever I looked down, no matter what was being said, I would smile, interpret the comment by writing something down, and look up again. It made the process more helpful: I had some control, I was doing a job. This was my professional demeanor. I began to enjoy the "criticism."

Gathering a consensus is part of a dramatic writer's job. Everyone has to take criticism, no matter what job you have. Most of us don't have to take our licks and praises in public. But dramatic writers do: it comes with the territory. Learn to do it gracefully, and when someone gives you a comment that can strengthen your work, consider it a gift. It is. That person is helping you.

After giving the draft to your five friends, see if there are any suggestions that you absolutely agree with. If several people commented on the same thing, it usually is a sign about the way that part is working. But you have to feel sure it's the right thing to do.

After I got over my initial defensiveness, I began to take another tack, which is equally unprofessional: trying to incorporate all criticism given to me. Who has the artistic vision then? No one! If something doesn't ring true to you, don't do it. Save the comments for future references, but don't ever do something that feels dreadfully wrong or confusing. Sift through the comments and find the ones that are helpful to you, confirming or refuting your initial reactions, and then utilize the precious new ideas that were given to you — that you know would help your project.

A final word about receiving criticism: sometimes it's clear that people have their own agendas with your work. This has more to do with them than with you. You still should listen to what they say. In the same way you wrote from your unique frame of reference, so an individual responds from a unique frame of reference, including personal agendas of all sorts. You still have to try to reach these people. Don't automatically discredit what they have to say. Listen to their points; sometimes help comes in ways you'd least expect it.

FIRST REVISION

You are now ready to do your first revision of the work. Incorporate some notes and make some of the work better. Revising involves two stages: "global" and "local." Global is when you make major structural changes: moving scenes around, taking characters out, changing the climax, etc. Local is more "polish" work; you change phrases, cut a few things, add a few lines. Make an attempt to fix the script on both levels, if possible, at this stage. (See exercises below.)

THE "COLD READING" STAGE

After you've completed the first revision, gather a group of friends together and read your script out loud. This is called a *cold reading*, meaning that it is unrehearsed and read by people basically unfamiliar with the work. If your friends are actors, great. If not, this is still a good way to start the "reading" process. Have a lot of food around; make a party of it. Tape record this rendition and let your friends give you some reaction to it afterwards. If there are any new criticisms, or if some of your writing problems are solved, take heart. You are making progress.

You should now pass the script on to professionals. (More about this in the marketing chapter.) Your goal will be to get a professional reading of your script, and then have a workshop performance of it, to gather more information about how it's working *and* to get a real audience's view of it.

You can see your job as a writer is becoming increasingly social; think of the people who come into contact with your project as resources and give them your respect. It will help you in the long run.

EXERCISES

1. DYNAMICS OF READINGS: Attend a reading of someone else's work (a famous person's, if possible): poetry, prose, play, screenplay, etc. Watch how the crowd receives the work. Listen to the comments made; see how it's presented. Make notes. How is it different from attending a fully-produced theatrical event?

2. GLOBAL: Gather your revision notes. Put any like comments together. Eliminate the notes that confuse you and/or make no sense. Make an outline of "global" revisions — structural changes that are necessary to make it better. Revise your first draft.

3. LOCAL: Now reread your draft for flow and dialogue. Take out dialogue/phrases that don't work. Revise locally. You are now ready for a cold reading.

16.
Formatting, Title, &
Copyright Guidelines

After you've finished your first draft, and after you've had an initial cold reading of it, you'll be ready to do revisions. At this point, it's prudent to start implementing a little pre-marketing strategy. I've composed a checklist that will help you finalize your manuscript before you begin to market it seriously. This should help you formulate any ideas that are of concern from a structural standpoint as well as from a professional, presentational one.

(The next two short sections are specifically about stage play formatting. For screenplays and teleplays, formatting is covered in Chapters 20 and 21. You may wish to skip ahead and then return to the Pre-Marketing Checklist on page 100.)

PRESENTATION OF YOUR PLAY

Every play should have a title page with the following information on it: the title of your play centered in the middle of the page, your name under it, a copyright statement on the lower left corner of the page, and contact information on the lower right corner of the page, including your phone number. (If you have an agent or representative, his or her number may go there instead.)

CAST LIST

The second page of your script should be a page that lists all pertinent information about the performance requirements of your play. You list all the cast members in the play and some identifying descriptions of them. You list the cast size and gender breakdown, the time and place of the play, the length, and any other optional information that you think is pertinent: the date of this draft, for instance; the production history of the readings; and the awards the play has received.

Your title page should look something like this:

```
                         TITLE OF PLAY
                              BY
                         YOUR NAME HERE


















                                     Your name
                                     Your address
                          Your area code and phone number



     C COPYRIGHT 1991 (or current year)
     by (your name here)
```

The following example is the cast page from my play *Lady-Like*, as a sample of how a cast/description page should look.

<u>LADY-LIKE</u>

CAST:

SARAH PONSONBY	An orphaned Irish girl
LADY ELEANOR BUTLER	An Irish lady
MARY CARRYLL	Sarah's maid

Cast Size: Three women
Time: The play begins in 1778 and spans fifty years.
Place: Ireland and Wales; points in between.
Length: A play in two acts; one intermission.

Third Draft Revision: 3/8/91

<u>LADY-LIKE</u> - History of readings and Finalist awards

1990 Association for Theatre in Higher Education,
Jane Chambers Award finalist.

Women in Theatre Reading, March 1990. Carpet Company Stage.

Maude Adams Award finalist, Stephens College, 1986.

PRE-MARKETING CHECKLIST

Script Basics

☐ Is the work neatly typed, error-free (no typos, no mechanical errors in the areas of usage, punctuation, and spelling)?
☐ Is it darkly printed on white, 8 1/2" by 11" inch paper?
☐ Is each page numbered?
☐ Is it properly formatted for the requirements of its form: stage play, screenplay, or teleplay?

Structure

☐ Is it clear who the work is about (protagonist)?
☐ Is the plot clear and unified?
☐ Is there conflict and action?
☐ Is there an event that transforms the leading character?

Character

☐ Are all the characters clearly revealed?
☐ Is there character consistency?
☐ Are main characters three-dimensional?
☐ Are secondary and tertiary characters three-dimensional?

Theme

☐ Does the work have a clear theme?
☐ Is the theme active in every scene?
☐ Is the theme stated/mentioned somewhere in your work, through dialogue?

Point of View

☐ Is the point of view used by the author clear, i.e., whose story is it? Whose eyes do we see it through — omniscient or a specific character's?
☐ Does the point of view further the overall effectiveness of each scene? Of the entire work?

Symbols and Metaphors

☐ Is the use of symbols clear and consistent?
☐ Is metaphor used in dialogue, too?

Setting

❑ Is the location of the script essential and effective?
❑ Does the setting open up the possibility of action?
❑ Does the setting have any metaphorical resonance?

Dialogue

❑ Is the dialogue natural in length of speeches (brevity in many responses) and sounds?
❑ Is all dialogue "character-specific"?
❑ Does all dialogue demonstrate a lexicon unique to each character who speaks it?

Title

❑ Do you have a working title? (See below for more details.)

Tone

❑ Is your tone clear?
❑ Is the tone consistent?

Humor and Irony

❑ Depending on your tone, is there an appropriate mix of humor and drama?
❑ If irony is used, is its function clear?

Overall Cohesiveness

❑ Do all the elements of the story work together to support a central purpose?

THE WORKING TITLE

I'm sure you already had some kind of title in mind for your script and have put it to use. This is called a "working title." However, now that you've had a chance to hear some reactions to your work, and probably to your title as well, it's time to consider your title as a marketing tool and signature.

Creating a good title, for any written work, is truly an art. It's a lot like writing poetry, I think, but it is very important from a commercial standpoint because it's going to be used to get people to read and come to your work. It sets the tone for the rest of your piece. A good title evokes mood. It should somehow encapsulate what your entire piece is about; it should be intriguing; it should be easy to pronounce. For example, the play *Greater Tuna*, a comedy about "the third smallest town in Texas," has an effective title. It's funny, it makes you wonder what it's about, and it describes the subject matter of the show.

I encourage you to pick a title that is reflective of your writer's voice. Many people overlook this important factor, but I always consider a title a sort of voice signature; it should be something that hasn't been used a lot, something with an original feel.

Provocative titles, when you first hear them, sound like they mean one thing, and by the time you've seen the work, you think it means something else: a double entendre or metaphor at work. I always attempt to find provocative titles that can function on a couple of levels.

In my play, *Telling Time*, about a storyteller who is raped, "Telling Time" is the name of her story hour presentation for children in a library. By the end of the play, we also know it was time in her life that she had to tell other people about her experiences or she wouldn't recover — from a psychological standpoint.

Another show of mine, a comedy entitled *Delicacies*, takes place in an elegant, magical restaurant of the same name. By the end, the audience knows that delicate matters between contemporary couples have been discussed: the real "delicacies" of the piece are the negotiations/feelings between women and men in our changing world.

Lady-Like is the title of my historical biography about the "Ladies of Llangollen" and their maid, who were definitely not considered "ladylike" in the Victorian era. It labels them as unconventional. However, by the end of the play, the audience knows that the show is also about the friendship that took place between these women: they liked each other, hence it denotes the exploration of female bonding as well.

TITLE REFINEMENT

Titles can be fragments of dialogue that are in your play, or they can strictly concept-based. Whatever your working title has been, take a look at it. See if you can polish it up, make it more unusual, or make it function on a couple of different levels. Does it set a mood? Before you market your work, make sure that the title is as good as you can make it. It is the first thing a reader will see. Make it work for you.

COPYRIGHTS AND REGISTRATION

In order to ensure that no one will steal your work, it is necessary to protect it through copyrights and registration. By placing the copyright statement on the title page of your script, you have initial protection against someone stealing your idea. You will then want to pursue a formal copyright. There are several ways to handle this procedure, but the best way is to use the Library of Congress Register of Copyrights or the Writers Guild of America.

Plays

In order to copyright your play, write to the Library of Congress, Register of Copyrights, Washington, DC 20559. Ask them to send you several copies of the appropriate form and the information you need to complete the form. Mail the completed form back to them with a copy of your play and the appropriate fee as soon as you receive it. Save your copyright certificate for the rest of your life.

Screenplays and Teleplays

Register screenplays and teleplays with the Writers Guild of America. Write or call them to inquire about appropriate fees for members and non-members. Check with the office nearest you.

Writers Guild of America (East)
555 W. 57th Street
New York, NY 10019
(212) 245-6180

Writers Guild of America (West)
8955 Beverly Blvd.
W. Hollywood, CA 90048
(213) 550-1000

The Guild will also send you a registration slip that confirms the deposit of your script with them. Save this as well.

I urge you to get started on this procedure immediately, but use the common-law copyright symbol on your material (as demonstrated in the last chapter) until you receive these slips.

As a professional, it is up to you to protect your work. Both of these organizations will give you more information about their functions and the legalities of protection if you ask for this information.

EXERCISES

1. Complete the Pre-Marketing Checklist.

2. Refine your title.

3. Write for registration forms today. Request extra information on copyright and registration.

17.
How to Market Plays

I hope you're holding a beautiful copy of your script in your hands. You should make several copies of it and put each copy in a stiff-paper three-hole binder, which you can get in most office supply stores.

Here's how marketing for the American theater works these days. Those Big Apple dreams are long gone. There are now large regional theaters, smaller regional houses, New York theaters (including shrinking Broadway and Off-Broadway markets), community theaters, and smaller theaters that fall somewhere in between, in terms of quality of productions, royalty payments, and professionalism.

As a playwright, you need to get produced at *any* theater to get started. Usually starting off at a smaller level and getting good reviews will enable you to get noticed by the larger regional theaters that pay the higher royalties and do the larger productions.

A production is the most validating thing that can happen to you. Anyone can sit around and write a play. You aren't truly a playwright until you've been produced and an audience has witnessed a production of your play. So that's your number one goal now that you've completed the initial writing process: getting a production. This can take almost as long as writing the play, if not longer. But it's crucial that you invest valuable time (and, I'm afraid, money) in putting your work out to the theater community.

Also, after you get a production, you'll want to keep track of all the press that your show gets: reviews, interviews that you do, interviews with any members of the cast or production team. You'll be able to make a press kit that can travel with the show as you try to market it in the future or get it published. Newspaper coverage is an excellent marketing tool for playwrights; keep track of all the ink that you get.

QUERY LETTERS

Here's how the process works. You'll start by sending out query letters to theaters that you've heard of (or use the list in the Appendix). This is your first marketing tool: a lively, one-page letter of inquiry addressed to the theater's literary manager. In this letter, you briefly introduce yourself as factually as possible (a little humor is okay but don't get too "cutesy"; this is a business letter, remember). Then, you describe your play and ask if they would like to read it. Mention that you'd like to be considered for production or any readings that they might have. You may enclose a self-addressed, stamped envelope for their response if you'd like to expedite the process but definitely include your address and phone number at the end of the letter.

A good query letter is the mark of a professional. Take care with it. Make it succinct. Proofread it. It should sell you in every way possible. This should be the beginning of a correspondence between you and a literary manager. Even if the literary manager writes back and says no, write again, expressing hope that he will read your next one.

You're trying to make connections; this is the social part of the writing process.

Here is a sample draft of a query letter describing my play, *Delicacies*.

```
Playwright's Name
Address
Date


Theater Company Name
Attn: Literary Manager
Address

Dear (Theater Company Name):
```

I am a Los Angeles playwright with a new play called DELICACIES that I'd like to submit to your theater. It's a two-act comedy about three married women who discover a magical restaurant called Delicacies.

In Act One, they invite men they work with to have dinner with them there. In Act Two, a few weeks later, they invite their husbands to the same restaurant — with surprising results.

In DELICACIES' 1990 premiere, the Los Angeles Times called it "a fascinating piece of theatrical trickery." Humorous in tone, with touches of surrealism, the play explores the nature of communication between contemporary couples.

The cast consists of 3 women and 4 men, with the men double-cast (friends/husbands). There is one set: a chic urban restaurant. The play's running time is about 2 hours.

Would you like to read DELICACIES? I'd be happy to send it to you. I can be reached at the address listed above or at (area code, phone number). I'd like to be considered for productions or readings at your theater.

Thank you for your consideration.

```
                              Sincerely,


                              Playwright's signature
                              Playwright's typed name
```

SYNOPSIS

They might write you back asking for a synopsis, a ten-page sample, and a résumé. Get those ready as marketing tools, too: pull your story from your exercise files (now you see why we did that!) and type it up as a synopsis.

Partial Synopsis Sample

Copyright 1990 by LAURA SHAMAS

DELICACIES - Synopsis
ACT ONE

Three married career women in their thirties, MERYL, KATE, and GLENDA, invite men they'd like to have affairs with to have dinner with them at DELICACIES restaurant. MERYL, a veterinarian, immediately regrets the risque arrangements, although it was her idea. KATE, an attorney, arrives with MERYL, and tries to calm her down. GLENDA, a sculptor, arrives dressed in revealing clothes and speaking unusually suggestive sexual innuendo.

Their "dates" are late: MERYL has invited DEREK, a veterinarian; KATE has invited MICHAEL, an attorney; GLENDA has invited KIERRAN, an artist. MERYL tries to get KATE and GLENDA to leave, before it's too late.

But then DEREK arrives, which proves to be an awkward scene. He's very sweet, but clearly does not know what to make of this arrangement. Next, KIERRAN arrives, carrying flowers for GLENDA. DEREK tries to discuss KIERRAN's art, a huge abstract painting called "Sucking Pink Balloons," but KIERRAN doesn't want to explain it. Finally, MICHAEL arrives; he's in a wildly loving mood, having just lost an important decision in court. The MAITRE D' serves unusual and magical entrees that suggest solutions to the problems in each of their lives.

Throughout the rest of the evening, tension followed by comic relief prevails, with the following character revelations:

1. GLENDA admits that she has caught her husband having an affair, thus explaining her bitterness. She also tells MERYL and KATE that she's afraid the lack of love in her life is ruining her art. She expresses a desperate need to find love again, to save herself and her work.

2. KATE becomes more confused as the evening progresses. She is used to being the "professional," and was going along with the theme of the evening in a semi-serious manner. She's never allowed herself to admit that she's

really unsatisfied with her marriage to FRANK: "I never see him. I never think about it." Her denial mechanism becomes increasingly evident; by assuming the leadership/caretaker role in every situation, she is consumed, able to avoid her own emotions and needs. She really doesn't even know what she wants with MICHAEL, who's divorced, although it's apparent what he wants with her (physical and emotional attraction). This becomes a point of conflict for KATE. She can't deny this as others witness it.

3. MERYL and DEREK get along beautifully. She puts forth the theory that women are able to get along better with men they work with because they share common interests — perhaps she was too young to marry in her early twenties — too young to have developed interests of her own. It is clear that DEREK respects her professionalism and MERYL loves that. She brings up the issue of children; he relates well to her worries about the biological time clock. But DEREK is innocent here, doing nothing suggestive, acting more like a platonic friend than a flirtatious lover.

The MAITRE D' continues to bring in a wonderful quirkiness: his service gets stranger and stranger, setting up the atmosphere of a magical place as opposed to a "realistic" restaurant. The act ends as KIERRAN and MICHAEL actually do bring up, in rather blunt ways, the idea of pairing up in some more formal way with GLENDA and KATE, respectively. MICHAEL asks KATE to marry him, and KIERRAN begs GLENDA to have an affair with him. DEREK and MERYL appear shocked as the entrees are served. END OF ACT ONE.

SAMPLE AND RÉSUMÉ

Pull the best ten pages from your script — the part that is most dramatic and has lots of action. Type up a résumé with your work experience, highlighting anything having to do with theater or writing.

When the theaters respond asking for your play, send in your script with a self-addressed, stamped envelope large enough for your play to fit into comfortably (10" by 13").

Spend an hour a day sending out plays. Spend two hours a day doing it if you can. It is vital that you get the play out. You won't be able to get an agent until you have some kind of track record: be your own agent initially. Believe in yourself enough to send out your work.

Once you send work out, you don't have to wait passively until you get a reply. You can enter contests (see the list below). An even better idea is to get involved with a local theater company — on any level. Human beings want to work with people they know and like. Join the ranks of a neighborhood theater group; it will help you become more familiar with the process of play production, and you might meet a few people who can help you network your play at a local level. Go to productions at this theater; support it. It will make you a better writer.

READINGS AND PRODUCTIONS

If you can get a public, staged reading from a theater company, rejoice. This is usually the first step all playwrights must take these days before getting a full production. Readings are marketing tools for the playwright as well as learning experiences about the scripts. You will really come away from the event with momentum; people will be talking about your work, you'll have seen it in front of an audience performed by actors. A director will have been very specific with you about what you were trying to do. Maybe you'll even have been to a few rehearsals. It's a wonderful first step.

One thing that's really helpful in a staged reading is to pare down your stage directions, which are usually read by a "narrator" to give a sense of the action of the play. It's amazing how long descriptions can slow down the pace of the reading: when it's acted out, it may go quickly. In order to give this "sleight-of-hand" illusion in a reading, edit out (with a pencil) about 50 to 75% of your stage directions for the public reading. Do it carefully but do it to ensure your reading will have an active pace.

Incorporate comments or ideas that you had about the reading into revisions. See if the theater would like to put the play into a workshop situation or perhaps even a full production. If they don't, find out why not. Maximize your contact with them: make sure they get to know you; find like-minded artists who might support your work in the future.

SENDING OUT THE SCRIPT

In order to start this process, in the Appendix is a list of theaters known to accept query letters from new writers. Address your queries to the literary manager. Many of them will not accept unsolicited scripts, but if they will, they'll inform you. Believe me, they'd much rather that you ask than just send it blindly. Also, start with a theater near you. It's wonderful if you can become associated with a theater where you live, as mentioned above. Phone numbers are included whenever possible, but don't call unless they ask you to. Most literary managers will get back to you as soon as they possibly can. If they have had your play forever with no response (nine to twelve months), a letter or call may be in order.

DRAMATISTS GUILD

When in doubt about any step of this process, a good organization to know about is The Dramatists Guild. With an interest in theater, you may join at the associate level. They provide a newsletter with contests and awards listed throughout the year, as well as the latest marketing and legal news. They also provide quarterlies with listings of theaters and contacts. They have a hotline for members with questions, too. I recommend joining immediately if you have a true interest in playwriting. The address is: The Dramatists Guild, 234 W. 44th Street, New York, NY 10036, (212) 398-9366.

For more theatrical marketing information, I suggest getting a copy of TCG's *Dramatists Sourcebook*, the most complete and up-to-date information on all current aspects of selling a play. See Recommended Reading for details.

AWARDS AND PRIZES

Most of the contests listed below require unproduced, unpublished submissions. *Write for complete guidelines.* Contests change a lot; it's better to get up-to-date information before you enter. Be sure to include a self-addressed, stamped envelope for their reply. Some contests charge an entry fee.

ADRIATIC AWARD; The International Society of Dramatists, U.S. Fulfillment Centre, Box 1310, Miami, FL 33153 (305) 674-1831. Material: Full-length plays, translations, adaptations, musicals. Deadline: November 1. Award amount: $250.

AMERICAN COLLEGE THEATER FESTIVAL; Michael Kanin Playwriting Awards Program, The John F. Kennedy Center for the Performing Arts, Washington, DC 20566 (202) 254-3437. Material: Awards for student-written plays, produced by universities (amounts vary). Deadlines are established by the region. Write for information: The ACTF Musical Award, Columbia Pictures Television Award for Comedy Playwriting, The David Library of the American Revolution Award for Playwriting on Freedom or Americana, The Lorraine Hansberry Playwriting Award, The National Student Playwriting Award, The Short Play Awards.

AMERICAN MUSICAL THEATRE FESTIVAL COMPETITION; Box S-3565, Carmel, CA 93921 (408) 625-5828. Fee. Material: Full-length musicals. Deadline: December 31. Award amount: $2,000 plus production.

ASF TRANSLATION PRIZE; The American-Scandinavian Foundation, 725 Park Avenue, New York, NY 10021 (212) 879-9779. Material: Translations. Deadline: June 3. Award amount: $1,000.

BAKER'S PLAYS HIGH SCHOOL PLAYWRITING CONTEST; Baker's Plays, 100 Chauncy Street, Boston, MA 02111 (617) 482-1280. Material: Full-length plays, one-acts, plays for young audiences. Deadline: January 30. Award amount: $500 and publication for first prize, $250 for second prize; third prize $100.

LUCILLE BALL FESTIVAL OF NEW COMEDY; American Vaudeville, Box 2619, Times Square Station, New York, NY 10108 (718) 204-5974. Material: Short comedies. Deadline: October 15. Award amount: $250, production, and expenses.

MARGARET BARTLE PLAYWRITING AWARD; Community Children's Theatre, 8021 East 129th Terrace, Grandview, MO 64030 (816) 761-5775. Material: Plays and musicals for young audiences. Deadline: January 27. Award amount: $500.

BEVERLY HILLS THEATRE GUILD — JULIE HARRIS PLAY-WRIGHT AWARD; 2815 North Beachwood Drive, Los Angeles, CA 90068 (213) 465-2703. Material: Full-length plays. Deadline: November 1. Award amount: $5,000 first prize, plus $2,000 to help finance production in Los Angeles area within one year; $1,000 second prize; $500 third prize.

SUSAN SMITH BLACKBURN PRIZE; 3239 Avalon Place, Houston, TX 77019 (713) 522-8529. Material: Full-length plays written in English by a woman playwright. Deadline: September 24. Award amount: $5,000; $1,000 for runner-up.

BLOOMINGTON PLAYWRIGHTS PROJECT CONTEST; 310 West 7th Street, Bloomington, IN 47404 (812) 334-1188. Material: Full-length plays. Deadline: October 15. Award amount: $250, production.

CAC NEW PLAY COMPETITION; Contemporary Arts Center, Box 30498, New Orleans, LA 70190 (504) 523-1216. Material: Full-length plays, plays for young audiences, musicals. Deadline: November 1. Award amount: $500 first prize; staged readings for top three works.

CALIFORNIA PLAYWRIGHTS COMPETITION; South Coast Repertory, Box 2197, Costa Mesa, CA 92628 (714) 957-2602. Material: Full-length plays by California residents. Deadline: November 1 (write for confirmation). Award amount: $5,000 first prize; $3,000 second prize; $2,000 third prize; production in theater's spring festival, travel, and expenses.

CALIFORNIA PLAYWRIGHTS PROJECT; Box 2068, San Diego, CA 92112 (619) 232-6188. Material: Full-length plays, one-acts, musicals by California writers. Deadline: to be announced. Award amount: $100, production or reading, travel expenses.

CHICANO LITERARY CONTEST; Department of Spanish and Portuguese, University of California at Irvine, Irvine, CA, 92717 (714) 856-5702. Material: One-acts by Chicano playwright or playwright who identifies strongly with Chicano community; unpublished play. Deadline: January 1. Award amount: $450 first prize; $300 second prize; $200 third prize (amounts may vary due to funding).

COLORADO CHRISTIAN UNIVERSITY NEW CHRISTIAN PLAYS COMPETITION; Department of Theatre, Colorado Christian University, 180 South Garrison Street, Lakewood, CO 80226 (303) 238-5386. Material: Full-length plays, one-acts, musicals, plays for young audiences of interest to Christian churches, colleges, or drama groups. Deadline: January 31. Award amount: $200; full workshop production or reading.

COLUMBIA ENTERTAINMENT COMPANY CHILDREN'S THEATRE PLAYWRITING CONTEST; 309 Parkade Blvd., Columbia, MO 65202 (314) 874-5628. Material: Plays and musicals for young actors. Deadline: June 30. Award amount: $250, production, expenses.

CORNERSTONE COMPETITION; The Penumbra Theatre Company, The Martin Luther King Bldg., 270 North Kent Street, St. Paul, MN 55102 (612) 224-4601. Material: Full-length plays dealing with the African-American experience. Deadline: February 15. Award amount: $1,000 plus workshop.

CHRISTINA CRAWFORD AWARDS; ATHE Playwrights Workshop, Theatre Arts Department, Humboldt State University, Arcata, CA 95521 (707) 826-3566. Material: Full-length plays, one-acts by enrolled college students; playwright must attend reading. Deadline: February 1. Award amount: $1,000 first prize; $500 second prize; $150 honorable mentions.

DAVIE AWARD FOR PLAYWRITING; GeVa Theatre, 75 Woodbury Blvd., Rochester, NY 14607 (716) 232-1366. Material: Full-length plays. Deadline: January 1. Award amount: $5,000 and production in festival.

DAYTON PLAYHOUSE PLAYWRITING COMPETITION; The Dayton Playhouse, 1301 East Siebenthaler Avenue, Dayton, OH 45414 (513) 277-0144. Material: Full-length plays. Deadline: November 30. Award amount: $1,000, possible production, travel expenses.

DEEP SOUTH WRITERS CONFERENCE; c/o English Department, Box 44691, University of Southwestern Louisiana, Lafayette, LA 70504. Material: Three competitions: 1) Miller Award, full-length plays dealing with English Renaissance and/or the life of Edward de Vere, Earl of Oxford. Deadline: July 15. Award amount: $1,500. 2) Paul T. Nolan One-Act Play Award. Material: One-acts for young and adult audiences. Deadline: July 15. Award amount: $200 first prize, $100 second prize, possible production. 3) Full-length play award. Material: Full-length plays, plays for young audiences. Deadline: July 15. Award amount: $300 first prize, $100 second prize.

DUBUQUE FINE ARTS PLAYERS, NATIONAL ONE-ACT PLAYWRITING CONTEST; 569 South Grandview Avenue, Dubuque, IA, 52001. (319) 582-5558. Material: One-acts. Deadline: January 31. Award amount: $200 first prize; $150 second prize; $100 third prize; production for all three plays.

DAVID JAMES ELLIS MEMORIAL AWARD; Theatre Americana, Box 245, Altadena, CA 91001. Material: Full-length plays not more than two hours long. Deadline: April 1. Award amount: $500 to best of four plays selected for production.

EMERGING PLAYWRIGHT AWARD; Playwrights Preview Productions, 1160 Fifth Avenue, #304, New York, NY 10029 (212) 996-7287. Material: Full-length plays, one-acts. Deadline: Ongoing. Award amount: $500, production, travel to attend rehearsals.

LAWRENCE S. EPSTEIN PLAYWRITING AWARD; 280 Park Avenue South, #22E, New York, NY 10010 (212) 979-0865. Fee. Material: Full-length plays, one-acts. Deadline: November 1. Award amount: $250.

FERNDALE REPERTORY THEATRE NEW WORKS COMPETITION; Box 892, Ferndale, CA 95536. Material: Full-length plays. Deadline: October 15. Award amount: $250, production with royalty.

FESTIVAL OF FIRSTS PLAYWRITING COMPETITION; Sunset Center, Box 5066, Carmel, CA 93921 (408) 624 3990. Fee. Material: Full-length plays. Deadline: August 31. Award amount up to $1,000, possible production. Fee. Material: full-length plays, one-acts. Deadline: November 1. Award amount: $250.

FESTIVAL OF SOUTHERN THEATRE PLAYWRITING COMPETITION; Department of Theatre Arts, University of Mississippi, University, MS 38677 (601) 232-5816. Material: Full-length plays by Southern playwrights or those who have plays with Southern themes. Deadline: November 30. Award amount: Three awards of $1,000 and production, expenses.

JOHN GASSNER MEMORIAL PLAYWRITING AWARD; New England Theatre Conference, 50 Exchange Street, Waltham, MA 02154 (617) 893-3120. Material: One-acts, plays for young audiences. Deadline: April 15. Award amount: $500 first prize. $250 second prize, staged reading at NETC annual convention.

GOLDEN GATE ACTORS ENSEMBLE PLAYWRIGHTS COMPETITION; Golden Gate Actors Ensemble, 580 Constanzo Street, Stanford, CA 94305 (415) 326-0336. Material: Full-length plays, series of one-acts. Deadline: June (TBA). Award amount: $1,000, staged reading.

HENRICO THEATRE COMPANY PLAYWRITING COMPETITIONS; The County of Henrico, Division of Recreation and Parks, Box 27032, Richmond, VA 23273 (804) 672-5100. Material: Two categories: one-acts on any subject and full-length plays about the Christmas season. Deadline: June 1. Award amount: $250 for one-acts; $200, production for full-lengths.

ROGER NATHAN HIRSCHL PLAYWRITING AWARD; Berkshire Theatre Festival, Box 797, Stockbridge, MA 02162 (413) 298-5536. Material: Full-length plays, one-acts. Deadline: October 1. Award amount: $3,000 commission, staged reading.

INNER CITY CULTURAL CENTER SHORT PLAY COMPETITION; 1308 South New Hampshire Avenue, Los Angeles, CA 90006 (213) 387-1161. Material: One-acts, translations, adaptations, plays for young audiences, musicals, operas. Deadline: August 10. Award amount: $1,500 first prize, $1,000 second prize, $500 third prize, or professional internships with studios.

JEWEL BOX THEATRE PLAYWRITING AWARD; 3700 North Walker, Oklahoma City, OK 73118 (405) 521-1786. Material: Full-length plays. Deadline: January 18. Award amount: $500, reading.

LOUISA KERN AWARD; Creative Writing Office, GN-30, University of Washington, Seattle, WA 98195 (206) 543-9865. Material: Short full-length plays, one-acts. Preference given to residents of the Northwest. Deadline: April 1. Award amount varies $1,900 to $2,500.

GEORGE R. KERNODLE PLAYWRITING CONTEST; Department of Drama, 406 Kimpel Hall, University of Arkansas, Fayetteville, AR 72701. Fee. Material: One-acts. Deadline: June 30. Award amount: $300 first prize, $200 second prize, $100 third prize.

MARC A. KLEIN PLAYWRITING AWARD; Department of Theatre, Case Western Reserve University, 2070 Adelbert Road, Cleveland, OH 44106 (216) 368-2858. Material: Full-length plays and one-acts. Deadline: April 1. Award amount: $500, production; $500 for travel and housing.

LEE KORF PLAYWRITING AWARDS; The Original Theatre Works, Burnight Center, Cerritos College, 11110 East Alondra Blvd., Norwalk, CA 90650 (213) 924-2100. Material: Full-length plays. Deadline: January 1. Award amount: $500 plus production.

KUMU KAHUA PLAYWRITING CONTEST; Department of Drama and Theatre, University of Hawaii at Manoa, 1770 East-West Road, Honolulu, HI 96822 (808) 948-7677. Material: Full-length plays, one-acts by Hawaii residents, related to Hawaiian experiences. Deadline: January 1. Award amount: $500 for full-length play; $200 for one-act.

LAMIA INK! INTERNATIONAL ONE-PAGE PLAY COMPETI-TION; Box 202, Prince Street Station, New York, NY 10012 (212) 978-4413. Material: One-page plays. Deadline: March 1. Award amount: $200, reading and publication.

HAROLD MORTON LANDON TRANSLATION AWARD; The Academy of American Press, 177 East 87th Street, New York, NY 10128 (212) 427-5665. Material: Published translations of verse dramas into English. Deadline: December 31. Award amount: $1,000.

LETRAS DE ORO SPANISH LITERARY PRIZE COMPETITION; University of Miami, 1531 Brescia Avenue, Coral Gables, FL 33124 (305) 284-3266. Material: Full-length plays, one-acts, adaptations, plays for young audiences, unpublished, written in Spanish. Deadline: October 12. Award amount: $2,500, publication.

LITTLE THEATRE OF ALEXANDRIA NATIONAL ONE-ACT PLAYWRITING COMPETITION; Little Theatre of Alexandria, 600 Wolfe Street, Alexandria, VA 22314 (703) 683-5778. Material: One-acts. Deadline: March 31. Award amount: $350 first prize, $250 second prize; $150 third prize, possible production.

LIVE OAK THEATRE NEW PLAY AWARDS; 311 Nueces Street, Austin, TX 78701 (512) 472-5143. Material: Full-length plays, one category for Texas playwrights. Deadline: November 1. Award amount: $1,000 for best new play; $1,000 for best Texas playwright, possible reading, workshop production.

LOVE CREEK ANNUAL SHORT PLAY FESTIVAL; 42 Sunset Drive, Croton-on-Hudson, NY 10520. Material: One-acts under forty-five minutes not produced in New York. Deadline: October 1. Award amount: Twelve or more finalists receive production; each compete for cash award of $300.

THE DENNIS MCINTYRE PLAYWRITING AWARD; Philadelphia Festival Theatre for New Plays, 3900 Chestnut Street, Philadelphia, PA 19104 (215) 222-5000. Material: Full-length plays by emerging playwright of conscience. Deadline: ongoing. Award amount: cash award TBA, production with travel and housing.

MERRIMACK REPERTORY THEATRE ANNUAL PLAYWRITING CONTEST; Box 228, Lowell, MA 01853 (508) 454-6324. Material: Full-length plays, translations, adaptations, plays for young audiences, musicals; resident of New England; dealing with the intellectual history of New England, women, and their role in the American workplace. Deadline: April 1. Award amount: $500 and workshop production to each of six finalists.

MIDSOUTH PLAYWRIGHTS' COMPETITION; Playhouse on the Square, 51 South Cooper Street, Memphis, TN 38104 (901) 725-0776. Material: Full-length plays, musicals. Deadline: April 1. Award amount: $500, production.

MILL MOUNTAIN THEATRE NEW PLAY COMPETITION; The Norfolk Southern Festival of New Works, Center in the Square; One Market Square, Roanoke, VA 24011 (703) 342-5730. Material: Full-length plays, one-acts. Cast limit of ten. Deadline: January 1. Award amount: $500, staged reading, travel stipend.

MIXED BLOOD VERSUS AMERICA; Mixed Blood Theatre Co., 1501 South 4th Street, Minneapolis, MN 55454 (612) 338-0937. Material: Full-length plays, musicals. Deadline: April 15. Award amount: $2,000, production.

MOVING TARGET THEATRE COMPETITION; Box 225794, Dallas, TX 75222 (214) 979-2599. Material: Full-length plays. Deadline: January 1. Award amount: $1,000, production with royalty; travel; room and board.

MRTW SCRIPT CONTEST; KOPN Radio, 915 East Broadway, Columbia, MO 65201 (314) 874-1139. Material: Short radio plays. Deadline: July 30. Award amount: $900 to be divided among three winners.

NATIONAL 10-MINUTE PLAY CONTEST; Actors Theatre of Louisville, 316 West Main Street, Louisville, KY 40202 (502) 584-1265. Materials: 10-minute plays. Deadline: December 1. Award amount: Heideman Award of $1,000; possible production with royalties.

"NEW PLAYS IN PROGRESS" PLAYWRIGHTS COMPETITION; The Production Company, Box 5352, Richmond, VA 23220 (804) 644-8990. Materials: Full-length plays, one-acts, translations. Deadline: February 1. Award amount: $1,000, production, travel, and housing.

NORTHERN NEW ENGLAND PLAYWRIGHTS AWARD; The Valley Players, Box 441, Waitsfield, VT 05673. Materials: Full-length plays by Northern New England residents. Deadline: August 1. Award amount: $1,000, possible production.

OGLEBAY INSTITUTE TOWNGATE THEATRE PLAYWRITING CONTEST; Oglebay Institute, Oglebay Park, Wheeling, WV 26003 (304) 242-4200. Materials: Full-length plays with simple sets. Deadline: January 1. Award amount: $300 plus production; up to $200 travel.

ROBERT J. PICKERING AWARD FOR PLAYWRITING EXCELLENCE; Coldwater Community Theatre, c/o 89 South Division, Coldwater, MI 49036 (517) 279-7963. Materials: Full-length plays. Deadline: November 30. Award amount: First prize $200; production and housing.

PLAYWRIGHTS' FORUM AWARDS; Theatreworks, University of Colorado, Box 7150, Colorado Springs, CO 80933 (719) 593-3232. Materials: One-acts. Deadline: December 1. Award amount: Two issued — $200; production; up to $350 travel to attend performance.

QRL POETRY SERIES AWARD; Quarterly Review of Literature, Princeton University, 26 Haslet Avenue, Princeton, NJ 08540 (609) 921-6976. Materials: Full-length plays, one-acts, translations. Deadline: Submissions accepted during November and May. Award amount: $1,000; publication in QRL Poetry Series. Up to five awards given a year for poetry and poetic drama.

FOREST A. ROBERTS/SHIRAS INSTITUTE PLAYWRITING AWARD; Forest A. Roberts Theatre, Northern Michigan University, Marquette, MI 49855 (906) 227-2553. Materials: Full-length plays, adaptations. Award amount: $1,000; production; travel, expenses for one-week residency.

SUMMERFIELD G. ROBERTS AWARD; The Sons of the Republic of Texas, 5942 Abrams Road, Suite 222, Dallas, TX 75231 (214) 343-2145. Materials: Full-length plays about living in the Republic of Texas. Deadline: January 15. Award amount: $2,500.

RICHARD RODGERS PRODUCTION AWARD; American Academy and Institute of Arts and Letters; 633 West 155th Street, New York, NY 10032 (212) 368-5900. Materials: Musicals. Deadline: November 2. Award amount: Production Award of up to $80,000 and/or Development Grants of up to $15,000 for professional readings.

LOIS AND RICHARD ROSENTHAL NEW PLAY PRIZE; Cincinnati Playhouse in the Park, Box 6537, Cincinnati, OH 45206 (513) 421-5440. Material: Full-length plays, related one-acts. Deadline: January 15. Award amount: $2,000 advance on royalties, production, $1,500 stipend, travel, room and board expenses for rehearsal periods.

SCHOLASTIC WRITING AWARDS; 730 Broadway, New York, NY 10003 (212) 505-3404. Materials: One-acts, radio, television, and film scripts by students in grades 7-12. Deadline: January 18. Award amount: Awards toward tuition ($1,000) and staged reading to winning high school senior, top 20 of other 50 receive cash awards of up to $125.

DOROTHY SILVER PLAYWRITING COMPETITION; Jewish Community Center of Cleveland, 3505 Mayfield Road, Cleveland Heights, OH 44118 (216) 382-4000. Materials: Full-length plays about the Jewish experience. Deadline: December 15. Award amount: $1,000, staged reading, possible production.

SOURCE THEATRE COMPANY NATIONAL PLAYWRITING COMPETITION; Source Theatre Company, 1835 14th Street NW, Washington, DC 20009 (202) 462-1073. Materials: Full-length plays, one-acts, musicals. Deadline: March 15. Award amount: $250, production in festival.

SOUTH CAROLINA NEW PLAY FESTIVAL; Trustus Theatre, Box 11721, Columbia, SC 29211 (803) 254-9732. Materials: Full-length plays, one-acts, plays for young audiences, written by South Carolina native, current or former resident, or have attended a South Carolina school. Deadline: April 1. Award amount: $1,000 first prize; $750 second prize; $500 third prize; production with travel and housing to attend rehearsals for first prize winner.

STANLEY DRAMA AWARD; Department of Humanities, Wagner College, 631 Howard Avenue, Staten Island, NY 10301 (718) 390-3256. Materials: Full-length plays, related one-acts, musicals recommended by teacher or theater professional. Deadline: September 1. Award amount: $2,000.

MARVIN TAYLOR PLAYWRITING AWARD; Sierra Repertory Theatre, Box 3030, Sonora, CA 95370 (209) 532-3120. Materials: Full-length plays, adaptations, musicals. Deadline: May 15. Award amount: $500, production.

UNICORN THEATRE NATIONAL PLAYWRIGHT AWARD (sliding dates); 3820 Main Street, Kansas City, MO 64111 (816) 531-7529. Materials: Full-length plays with contemporary themes and settings, prefer social relevance. Deadline: Ongoing. Award amount: $1,000, possible production.

VIRGINIA PRIZE FOR PLAYWRITING; Virginia Commission for the Arts, James Monroe Bldg., 17th Floor, 101 North 14th Street, Richmond, VA 23219 (804) 225-3132. Materials: Full-length plays by professional playwrights who reside in Virginia. Deadline: January 15. Award amount: $10,000.

THEODORE WARD PRIZE FOR PLAYWRITING; Columbia College Chicago Theater/Music Center; 72 East 11th Street, Chicago, IL 60605 (312) 663-9462. Materials: Full-length plays, translations, adaptations. Deadline: July/August TBA. Award amount: First prize $2,000 and production; second prize $500 and staged reading.

L. ARNOLD WEISSBERGER PLAYWRITING COMPETITION;
New Dramatists, 424 W. 44th Street, New York, NY 10036
(212) 757-6960. Materials: Full-length plays. Deadline:
February 1. Award amount: $5,000.

WEST COAST ENSEMBLE FULL-LENGTH PLAY COMPETI-
TION; Box 38728, Los Angeles, CA 90038 (213) 871-8673.
Materials: Full-length plays. Deadline: November 1. Award
amount: $500, production, royalty on any performance be-
yond a six-week run.

ANN WHITE NEW PLAYWRIGHTS COMPETITION; 5266 Gate
Lake Road, Ft. Lauderdale, FL 33319 (305) 722-4371. Deadline: November 15. Award amount: $500 plus production.

WICHITA STATE UNIVERSITY PLAYWRITING CONTEST;
University Theatre, Wichita State University, Box 31, Wichita,
KS 67208 (316) 689-3185. Materials: Full-length plays, one-
acts by students currently enrolled at U.S. college, ninety
minutes minimum. Deadline: February 15. Award amount:
Production, expenses for playwright to attend production.

YOUNG PLAYWRIGHTS FESTIVAL; The Foundation of the
Dramatists Guild, 234 West 44th Street, New York, NY 10036
(212) 575-7796. Materials: Full-length plays, one-acts written
by playwrights under the age of nineteen. Deadline: October
1. Award amount: Staged reading or production with royalty,
travel, and residency, one-year Dramatists Guild membership.

18.
Agents, Publishers, & Producers

The next steps in marketing a play after getting a production or award are: 1) to try to get it published, or 2) to try to get it commercially produced, 3) to try to get a grant or some sort of financial support, and 4) to find an agent to promote the whole endeavor.

AGENTS

It is increasingly difficult for playwrights to find agents. By comparison, there is much more money to be made in film and television, so fewer and fewer agents represent playwrights solely for the theatre. Also, it's kind of a Catch-22 situation: most agents don't want to represent you until you have a track record, and it's hard to get a track record without an agent.

What are you supposed to do? First, you should try to get productions on your own, as mentioned previously. Establish your own ties with theaters, directors, literary managers, other writers, producers, state art agencies, and publishers. Most writers will tell you that you land your own jobs anyway, through contacts that you make yourself.

If you've been lucky enough to land a production of your play, you can actively seek publication, future production, and grant funds. After succeeding in these arenas, it becomes easier to find an agent.

If you'd like to know more about what an agent can or cannot do, you can get a free pamphlet on the subject from the Society of Authors' Representatives, 10 Astor Place, 3rd Floor, New York, NY 10003. Be sure to include a self-addressed, stamped envelope. The Dramatists Guild has a current list available as well (234 W. 44th Street, New York, NY 10036). I highly recommend both of those sources. Then, ask other theater artists what they think; often they will recommend agents they like or with whom they have worked. Literary managers are often excellent sources for agent referrals, too.

PUBLISHERS

The beauty of publication is you don't have to spend all your time photocopying once the play is published. The play makes money while someone else promotes it through a catalog (this is part of the publisher's job). The publisher can often act like an agent in getting the word out about you; publication is prestigious so it validates your work enormously.

It is always better to have proof of production before sending your play to a publisher. A few will have a look at unproduced plays, especially in the educational market. But if you've got reviews (those excellent marketing tools), send them, along with a query letter, to publishers, asking if they'll read your work. Again, as with theaters, you are trying to make contacts! If they write you back requesting your work, send it immediately with a large, self-addressed, stamped envelope.

If you get a rejection letter, write back to them, telling them how much you appreciate the time they took to read your work. This rejection opens the door for a future job as well; this happened to me with my very first play. One publishing company wrote back an extensive two-page rejection letter. I remembered it and wrote back. A correspondence was established — even a friendship. Two years later they published a children's play I wrote. It can happen to you too. Take any written response as genuine interest; it is.

List of Publishers

Amelia Magazine, 329 "E" Street, Bakersfield, CA 93304 (805) 323-4064. Types: One-acts. Send script and evidence of any production. Fee. Prize deadline of May 15. Notifies in two months. Payment: $150 prize, complimentary copies.

American Theatre, Theatre Communications Group, 355 Lexington Avenue, New York, NY 10017 (212) 697-5230. Types: Full-length plays, one-acts, translations, etc. Major work from current theater scene. Submission at editor's request. Payment: Negotiated fee, complimentary copies.

The Americas Review, University of Houston, 4800 Calhoun, Houston, TX 77004 (713) 749-4768. Types: Unpublished works of any kind in English or Spanish by Hispanic writers only. Notifies in three months. Payment: Fee and complimentary copies.

Anchorage Press, Box 8067, New Orleans, LA 70182 (504) 283-8868. Types: Works for young audiences of any kind. Plays should be produced at least three times. Include proof of production. Notifies in 1½ to 3 months. Payment: Royalty.

Aran Press, 1320 South 3rd Street, Louisville, KY 40208 (502) 636-0115. Types: Full-length plays, one-acts, translations. Plays for community theater, college or university, summer stock, dinner theater, and professional theater. Prefers letter of inquiry. Notifies in three weeks. Payment: 10% book royalty, 50% production royalty, playwright contributes to publishing costs, $200 for full-length plays, $100 for one-act.

Art Craft Play Company, Box 1058, Cedar Rapids, IA 52406 (319) 364-6311. Types: Full-length plays, one-acts, musicals for junior and senior high school market. Notifies in two months. Payment: Negotiated royalty or payment, complimentary copies.

Baker's Plays, 100 Chauncy Street, Boston, MA 02111 (617) 482-1280. Types: Full-length plays, one-acts, plays for young audiences, chancel dramas, musicals; prefer plays suitable for high school, community, and regional theater. Notifies in three to four months. Payment: Royalty.

The Bellingham Review, The Signpost Press, 1007 Queen Street, Bellingham, WA 98226. Types: One-acts, preferably under 5,000 words. Notifies in two to three months. Payment: One complimentary copy and one-year subscription.

Broadway Play Publishing, 357 W. 20th Street, New York, NY 10011 (212) 627-1055. Types: Full-length plays, prefer original, innovative work by American playwrights. Notifies in three months. Payment: 10% book royalty, 80% amateur royalty, 90% stock royalty; ten complimentary copies.

Brooklyn Review, Department of English, Brooklyn College, Brooklyn, NY 11210 (718) 780-5195. Types: One-acts of not more than ten pages in length. Notifies in six weeks to six months. Payment: Two complimentary copies.

Callaloo, Department of English, University of Virginia, Wilson Hall, Charlottesville, VA 22903 (804) 924-6637. Types: One-acts for journal of Afro-American and African arts and letters published by John Hopkins University Press. Notifies in six months. Payment: Complimentary copies and offprints; payment when grant money is available.

I.E. Clark, St. John's Road, Box 246, Schulenburg, TX 78956 (409) 743-3232. Types: Full-length plays, one-acts, translations, musicals, plays for young audiences; prefers produced work. Notifies in three to six months. Payment: book and performance royalties.

Contemporary Drama Service, Meriwether Publishing, Ltd., 885 Elkon Drive, Colorado Springs, CO 80907. Types: Full-length plays, one-acts, plays for young audiences, musicals, readers' theater, monologues for teenage, high school, and college market, prefers comic, produced work. Notifies in two months. Payment: Book and performance royalties or payment for amateur and publishing rights.

Drama Book Publishers, 260 Fifth Avenue, New York, NY 10001 (212) 725-5377. Types: Full-length plays, translations, musicals; professionally produced plays only — Broadway, etc. Notifies in several months. Payment: Advance against royalties.

The Dramatic Publishing Company, 311 Washington Street, Box 109, Woodstock, IL 60098 (815) 338-7170. Types: Full-length plays, one-acts, translations, adaptations, plays for young audiences, musicals. Prefers produced plays. Notifies in two to four months. Payment: Standard royalty; ten complimentary copies, 30% discount on additional copies.

Dramatics Magazine, 3368 Central Parkway, Cincinnati, OH 45225 (513) 559-1996. Types: Full-length plays, one-acts for educational theater magazine, prefer produced plays for high school production. Notifies in six weeks. Payment: One-time publication rights, complimentary copies.

Dramatists Play Service, 440 Park Avenue South, New York, NY 10016 (212) 683-8960. Types: Full-length plays, one-acts, translations, adaptations, plays for young audiences, musicals, prefer work produced in New York City. Notifies in two weeks. Payment: Advance against royalties, 10% book royalty, 80% amateur royalty, 90% stock royalty, ten complimentary copies.

Eldridge Publishing Company, Drawer 216, Franklin, OH 45005 (513) 746-6531. Types: Full-length plays, one-acts, musical plays for school, church, and community theater, Christmas plays, junior/senior high school musicals. Notifies in two months. Payment: Outright purchase, percent of royalties or percent of sales, complimentary copies.

Encore Performance Publishing, Box 692, Orem, UT 84057 (801) 225-0605. Types: Full-length plays, one-acts, translations, adaptations, plays for young audiences, musicals that have had at least two amateur or professional productions; special interest in work with family, holiday, or Christian messages. Notifies in six to eight weeks. Payment: 10% book royalty, 50% performance royalty, two complimentary copies.

Freelance Press, Box 548, Dover, MA 02030 (508) 785-1260. Types: Musicals for young audiences only, issue-oriented, classical adaptations, one hour long, performances by and for young people. Notifies in three months. Payment: 10% book royalty, 66% performance royalty, one complimentary copy.

Samuel French, 45 West 25th Street, New York, NY 10010 (212) 206-8990. Types: Full-length plays, one-acts, plays for young audiences, musicals; prefers script format presented in "Guidelines" booklet (write for information and cost). Notifies in two to twelve months. Payment: Advance against royalties, 10% book royalty, 80% amateur royalty, 90% stock royalty, ten complimentary copies.

Greatworks Play Service, Box 3148, Shell Beach, CA 93448 (805) 773-3419. Types: Full-length plays, one-acts, translations, adaptations, musicals; write for guidelines. Notifies in one to six months. Payment: Production royalty (75% professional, 50% amateur).

Heuer Publishing Company, Box 248, Cedar Rapids, IA 52406 (319) 364-6311. Types: Full-length plays, one-acts, musicals for junior/senior high school market. Notifies in two months. Payment: Royalty or payment for amateur rights; complimentary copies.

Lillenas Drama Resources, Lillenas Publishing Company, Box 419527, Kansas City, MO 64141 (816) 931-1900. Types: Full-length plays, one-acts, plays for young audiences, musicals, collections of sketches, etc., with Christian themes. Write for guidelines. Notifies in two to three months. Payment: Purchase or royalty.

Modern International Drama, Theatre Department, State University of New York-Binghamton, Box 6000, Binghamton, NY 13901 (607) 777-2704. Types: Translations; guidelines sent on request. Notifies in one month. Payment: Three complimentary copies of biannual journal.

New Plays, c/o Patricia Whitton, 108 Park Lane, Charlottesville, VA 22901. Types: Plays for young audiences, produced, innovative material. Notifies after one to two months. Payment: 10% book royalty, 50% production royalty.

Out/Look National Lesbian and Gay Quarterly, 2940 16th Street, Room 319, San Francisco, CA 94103 (415) 626-7929. Types: One-acts for quarterly journal publishing one to two plays a year; plays under 4,000 words long with gay or lesbian content. Notifies in three months. Payment: Fee and complimentary copies.

PAJ Publications/*Performing Arts Journal*, 131 Varick Street, Suite 902, New York, NY 10013 (212) 243-3885. Types: Full-length plays, one-acts, translations; international arena. Submit query letter. Notifies in one to two months. Payment: Royalty and/or fee.

Pioneer Drama Service, Box 22555, Denver, CO 80222 (303) 759-4927. Types: Full-length plays, plays for young audiences, musicals, holiday plays; produced work for educational market. Notifies in two to six weeks. Payment: Outright purchase or royalty.

Players Press, Box 1132, Studio City, CA 91604 (818) 789-4940. Types: Full-length plays, one-acts, translations, adaptations, plays for young audiences, short plays, teleplays, screenplays; produced work. Notifies in one to six months. Payment: Royalty, purchase, option, complimentary copies.

Plays in Process, Theatre Communications Group, 355 Lexington Avenue, New York, NY 10017 (212) 697-5230. Types: Full-length plays, one-acts, translations, adaptations, plays for young audiences, musicals. U.S. author produced by TCG theater during current season and nominated by artistic director or literary manager. Annual deadline. Notifies in three months. Payment: Script circulation to theatrical subscribership; ten complimentary copies.

Scripts and Scribbles, 141 Wooster Street, New York, NY 10012 (212) 473-6695. Types: Full-length plays, one-acts, texts, or performance art pieces; publishes nontraditional theater pieces and work produced outside NYC. Notifies in six months. Payment: Twenty-five complimentary copies.

GRANTS

Another way to support your playwriting habit is to get funding from foundations and agencies. There are several avenues available to playwrights through private sources, service organizations, and state agencies. The National Endowment for the Arts grants playwriting monies for professionally produced writers; you can write for more information from the NEA Theater Program Fellowship for Playwrights at 1100 Pennsylvania Avenue NW, Washington, DC 20506 or call (202) 682-5425. The Dramatists Guild can be of help in this area, too; it has a list of foundations that give grants to dramatists.

But don't overlook support at the local level. The city you live in may give artists grants. In 1987, I received an artistic fellowship from the City of Denver Commission on Cultural Affairs, and it was quite a thrill. Any time a mayor gives you something it's exciting, but to think that the city where I lived was giving me artistic support to write something for the theater — what an inspiration creatively and financially. Check out your city's arts/cultural commission to see what programs they offer. If your city has such a commission, you'll find the number in your phone book.

Finally, the state is a good resource for artistic grants. Write to your state's art agency. At the very least, you should request to be on their mailing list. Write and find out what they offer playwrights on an annual or biannual basis. Ask them for a list of other foundations in your state that support playwrights.

Getting involved with your state council, through programs or panels, is an effective way of meeting other artists, who can also direct you to other means of creativity and support. Volunteering for an arts council function or service is an excellent way to learn about how councils are run and who they support. Altruism aside, it can be a very educational experience and one most playwrights benefit from.

PRODUCERS

There are producers who are interested in commercial material that can transfer to major markets in the theater — notably London, New York, Chicago, L.A., San Francisco, etc. A theatrical agent will usually have producer contacts and will try to get your work seen by producers who would be able to take a work into a major market. Many commercial producers will only look at plays recommended by a theater professional or an agent they know.

But if you don't have an agent, *and* if you have good press for your show, you can send out reviews, a synopsis, and a good cover letter to producers, asking them to read your script. If your letter is lively and your reviews favorable, many will want at least to give your show a read.

If possible, invite producers to come and see your show while it's running. Sometimes people will ask to see videotapes but usually the quality is such that it really doesn't capture the essence of how your work played in front of an audience. Try to entice them to see it live; tell them how long your show is running and that you'll be happy to arrange for tickets.

The Dramatists Guild's Quarterly lists commercial producers who are currently looking at projects. The addresses and phone numbers of the producers are furnished with the producers' approval. Contact the Dramatists Guild for the most current list of producers.

19.
Working with Directors, Actors, & Designers

Once you get into a production situation, you will be working with other artists. In essence, you will collaborating with them; they will be interpreting your work and finding ways to realize your thoughts, dreams, and words. Of course, they will be offering new insights and observations about your script. They may even present ideas that they think are better than what you've written, in an effort to improve the project.

CREATING WORKING RELATIONSHIPS

Because of this process, many dramatic writers get into adversarial relationships with other artists. For some reason, they decide that unless a piece is performed exactly as they envision it, it is wrong.

I'm a fairly headstrong individual (I'm a writer). In the past, I've been emphatic about the way in which my work was interpreted. I urge other writers to show passion and interest in how their work is treated.

But there is a way to make your ideas known and still maintain an open, working environment with those around you. Instead of functioning on your own, try to think about forming partnerships — creative partnerships.

It's to the writer's advantage to work hand in hand with other artists. This is a partnership, after all; you're all working on the same thing — your script. By putting your energy into sharing a vision, instead of fighting for supremacy, you can strive to make something work. Try a little team spirit.

If you hear some suggestions that you think would actually improve your work, take them with an air of grace.

Use them; think of it as help because it is help. Sometimes it's given to us when all we want is praise, but it is help, nonetheless.

DIRECTORS

Directors mount the script for a specific arena. Depending on what dramatic form you're writing in, this means you can expect different levels of presentational expertise. But it always means a vision is presented — either on a stage or through a camera. There is a definite visual orientation, and with this will come a sense of style and pace that you might not have had originally.

Obviously, this may be a somewhat different view than you had as the writer. What can you learn from it? You can definitely learn more about the medium you're writing for, and you can learn how "produceable" your script is based on the ideas the director has. Some of this will be based on dramaturgy as well as practical considerations.

I have learned so much from directors in the last few years; they have shown me better structures, and they've shown me that much of what I write works well. They've pointed out weak character traits and inconsistencies; they've praised strong characters in action. But they've really helped me learn more about my writing. A good director is a great asset to a writer. Find one who speaks your language.

In your initial meeting with a director, have a specific set of criteria that you want to go over in regards to your work. Think of it as a job interview that works both ways. Try to figure out if you can work with the director (personality-wise), but also see if you come close to sharing the same view of the work (artistically). If possible, see samples of work of anyone with whom you're considering working. If you feel you're too far apart in any aspect, respectfully say that you're talking to a few other people and then proceed to do so.

Never enter into a situation that you feel uncomfortable with from the beginning. It will only get worse. That's the nature of high drama.

ACTORS

Respect actors. They're up there making what you wrote come to life. They're the ones who have to face the public in one form or another. They're trying to breathe life into your words. They make your work three-dimensional.

However, know that many actors look at the project from the viewpoint of the character they're playing; after all, that's their main concern, their job. This will sometimes lead to an imbalanced judgment of your work. You've got to be able to listen to their suggestions, about things from individual lines to blocking to act structures, and know that the responsibility for maintaining the arc of the whole script rests on *your* shoulders, not theirs. Keep the big picture in mind as you hear the suggestions that come your way. Stay strong in your vision. I'm not saying you won't receive some wonderful ideas; from my experience, I can almost promise you that you *will* get some great revision inspiration, so stay alert. Rehearsals and performances are extraordinarily creative times for all artists. But ultimately it's your name on the piece. Take the reins. Weigh all suggestions against the excellent foundations that you've established through your writing process.

DESIGNERS

I can't stress enough the importance of your collaboration with designers. The technical knowledge that you can glean from designers — no matter what medium you're working in — is immense. And this can affect future writing projects as well the one you're currently working on.

Let designers give you their vision for what you have outlined in your script. Listen to the practical details about how lights, sound, sets, props, costumes, etc., will function. Think about how the technical elements highlight your script. Is there a way for you to utilize the elements even more effectively? Do they have a better idea for a set? If so, would it work metaphorically for your theme, etc.? This is one of the most creative aspects of mounting any script. Many beginning writers mistakenly focus on acting as the most important aspect of production. But every aspect is equally important to the artistic vision (although box-office appeal may dictate otherwise).

SHOULD YOU DIRECT YOUR OWN WORK? SHOULD YOU STAR IN YOUR OWN PROJECT?

Do you have a strong stomach? Lots of energy? The ability to divorce yourself from the writing to critique it and listen to others' honest opinions of it? Can you say your own line and figure out if it works? Are you a wunderkind? If not, then I'd stay away from directing or acting in your own work for awhile. (If that's the only way you can get it produced, and you've been trying for over a year, and you've got some previous experience, then it's possible . . . and good luck.)

You lose that collaborative edge when you take on several hats. It's hard to listen to something you wrote if you're the one saying it. If you want to learn about writing as quickly as possible, write and stand back. See what happens. Get some perspective. Find out about the process.

Of course, there are many examples of artists working on stage and especially on screen who do all these things at once. They write and direct; write, direct, and act; write and act; write and produce, etc. I recommend that you try your hand at these activities in individual instances until you achieve a level of mastery in one or more area. After all, it's your name on the work. You want it to have the best possible airing.

20.
How to Structure a Screenplay

In a screenplay, you tell a story with moving pictures.

Even though it seems obvious when you think about it, many people forget that theater, film, and television are all part of the same kind of writing: dramatic performance. Film and television are modern variations of dramatic form, and developed out of a merging of theater and photography: moving pictures. As we discussed in the third chapter, the audience is the focal point for all dramatic presentation. Because of this, the same dramatic principles exist in all three forms but manifest themselves in different ways. So while there are commonalities, there are sophisticated, striking differences, too.

In other words, in film, you must still create a protagonist (and other characters) who changes through a series of conflicts and rising action that form a plot. These scenes have variety in locale and characters. The Act Two climax scene should be an explosive one that involves your protagonist and an antagonist.

Of course, you must have a strong theme, excellent settings, and appropriate "character-specific" dialogue at work. Every scene moves your protagonist's story forward; every scene is a stride towards your protagonist's goal. But in movies, you tell your story in about 25 to 30 scenes, averaging 3 to 5 pages in length. The whole script should total 100 to 120 pages.

BASIC BLUEPRINT

There are invisible act delineations in a film script (but these are not stated in the script). It has the flow of one seamless, whole piece. As mentioned in Chapter 7, a screenplay is a three-act form (evolving from the old three-act play). As you write it, you should be aware of this basic blueprint: Pages 1-30 comprise Act One (six or more scenes with a significant circumstance that arises at the end to propel the protagonist into the second act); 30-90 make up the Second Act (about fifteen scenes — major obstacles with extreme peril and near defeat around page 75 resulting in a big climax that the hero/heroine must overcome); Act Three is pages 90 to 120 and includes the resulting falling action from the Act Two climax (6 to 8 scenes), and finally, protagonist transformation must occur.

This, in the most basic and general sense, is the structure of a screenplay. Certainly, film is a fascinating art form in and of itself; if you are serious about screenwriting, I encourage you to read as many screenplays as possible, see as many films as you can, and read books about film structure and film-making. Read a screenplay and then rent the movie, following along as you watch it. It is worthy of complete study.

Without being too formulaic, here are some primary guidelines about a screenplay:

CHARACTER AND SETTING

Pick your protagonist in the same careful way discussed in Chapter 5. But know that you will have the fun task of surprising the audience with differences in locales and clothes and more variety in visuals. Have fun with spectacle; think of each scene as a picture you're framing. Pick settings of interest and metaphoric resonance.

PROTAGONIST/ANTAGONIST RELATIONSHIP

Classically, you need an antagonist to counteract your protagonist. This, too, was discussed earlier and you might wish to review it. In movies, the antagonist helps move the action forward and give our hero/heroine clear obstacles to overcome. The more three-dimensional your antagonist, the more heightened the tension; the better the battle.

STORY OUTLINE, THEME

You should begin with a character and action plan, an outline of about 25-30 scenes (this can also serve as the basis for a *treatment*, a narrative description of the story of your movie). Again, know your theme. Know what transformation you want your protagonist to achieve. As you make this outline, circle the end of Act One and Act Two points; be sure that the climaxes there are big enough to carry the story into the next part of the film.

SUB-PLOTS

Sub-plots, secondary storylines that somehow resonate or amplify your primary plot, should also be included. These may involve the allies of the protagonist or lesser characters in the script. The sub-plot should never compete with the main plot; the crisis should never be as important as the primary story. But it may parallel it; it may have a different outcome than your main story — thus further delineating the protagonist's glory.

SCENE STRUCTURE

As we discussed earlier, a scene contains conflict and action. Start all scenes at action points. Begin them in the middle of action; let your action provide exposition (*backstory*), character, and dialogue all at once. The same "rising action" dynamic of scene-building applies in film (review Diagram #1 on page 42). Each scene must begin at a higher point than the previous scene. With film you have the luxury of really jumping around, which can heighten suspense and interest. Tell a story with images. Give us the best essence of each scene; nothing in the scene should be extraneous — only cut crystal. Think of each scene as a refined jewel (then the whole script is treasure!). Don't include anything self-indulgent or unnecessary; the audience should see pure character in motion. Keep all your scenes to around five pages.

DIALOGUE

Remember, you're moving pictures; don't get too wordy. Make sure that your dialogue is natural-sounding, brief, in the common vernacular of your characters. We rarely talk in complete sentences. When in doubt, "show us, don't tell us."

SPECIAL EFFECTS

For budgetary considerations, try to keep special effects usage down. Try to keep exotic locales to a minimum. Yes, it's that old paradox; write a spectacle but write it cheaply. Be creative — the pressure is on.

NARRATIVE DESCRIPTION

You will need description to suggest locales and other physical information. This should be kept to a minimum — again, the cut crystal/jewel idea: how to say something as cleanly as possible and still get across a mood, a place, a time, a unique, real atmosphere ... This is the sort of descriptive challenge you face in a screenplay. It is also formatted in a specific manner.

COMMERCIALISM

What of elements of romance, sex, violence, and other obvious ingredients of popular films? What ingredients make a screenplay saleable? In the very first chapter, I asked you to evaluate the current marketplace. I'm sure you still have those notes. There are definite trends at play at the box office; however, it's your decision whether or not you need to use that information to influence what happens in your screenplay. I'm still a firm believer in writing from your heart — from the seeds of passion and truth, beauty grows (or something like that). Your name will be on it (at least at first). Make your work something you believe in and worry about salability later.

FORMAT

Using the right format and technical terms often overwhelms beginning screenwriters. Once you get it down, you'll do it by habit, instinctively, so just try to get the basics of it. I've included sample pages to show how a screenplay should look. For practice, you can type the page over yourself a couple of times to get the hang of it.

Briefly, here are the guidelines for screenplay preparation that you would use if you were submitting your screenplay for consideration of industry professionals (not a final shooting script):

1. Use $8^1/2$" by 11" white paper. Bind it with covers and brads. You need a title page, with the title and your name in the center, and your or your representative's contact information in the lower righthand corner.

2. Start with

```
FADE IN:
```

(just like that next to the lefthand margin).

3. Begin stage directions 2 inches from the left edge of the paper.

```
"INT. CHURCH SANCTUARY - DAY"
```

This is a slug line or information line. It should always be in caps; the information is always the same: "Interior" or "Exterior" information, the shot if you're specifying it, the location and time (day/night).

4. Description follows immediately below the information line. The description should be a visual one. Character names are centered at $4^1/2$ inches in from the left. Dialogue starts at 3 inches from the left, and should not extend beyond $2^1/2$ inches from the right edge of the paper. Character names are capitalized the first time they're mentioned, for casting purposes. (However, you do not have to capitalize secondary or lesser characters who don't have any lines.) So putting it together, it might look like this:

```
INT.  CHURCH SANCTUARY - DAY

A priest, TOMASA, enters carrying a large velvct
sack that is filled with money.  He approaches the
```

empty pews. Suddenly, he drops the bag and money
spills all over the floor. He drops to his knees,
gathering up the cash as quickly as possible.

                    TOMASA

          Why is he coming now? It was supposed to

          be tomorrow.

                                          CUT TO:

5. Double space between dialogue and scene description. Single space between lines of scene description. At the end of a scene you can write CUT TO: or DISSOLVE TO: (can mean time has passed), placing the words on the right, for emphasis, although this is assumed for the most part when a new scene begins.

6. When a character's speech continues from one page to the next, indicate as such to the actors by writing (MORE) on the line under the last sentence, indented to the same margins as the character's name. Then, put the character's name and (CONT'D) on top of the next page.

7. Shot descriptions should be basic; let a director decide how to shoot something. As the writer, you should focus on what you want the camera to see in a general sense. Avoid excessive camera directions. Keep it to the "big picture." You can specify a close shot (CLOSE ON) if you need to see something specially or ANGLE ON if a different point of view will help. But usually, a "master shot" will suffice.

8. Here are some other things that are capitalized in screenplays: AD LIB (when actors create incidental dialogue — spontaneous, "of-the-moment" variety); VOICE OVER (V.O.) — when there's spoken narration; OFFSCREEN (O.S.) — the character speaks but is just offscreen; TITLES OF BOOKS, TITLES OF SONGS; BEGIN and END TITLES (when the main credits start and end).

For more information, consult *The Complete Guide to Standard Script Formats, Part One, The Screenplay* by Cole and Haag, published by CMC Publishing (1980).

The following sample pages are from my screenplay *Unnatural History*. These will give you more of an idea of how the format should look. Again, for practice, you can type these a few times yourself to get the hang of it.

The page shown here is near the end of the screenplay. Just to fill you in: In this comic fantasy, two women scientists discover unicorns in Alaska. They try to take the creature to a convention of scientists in San Francisco, and the unicorn, named Mac, escapes. Another scientist tries to capture their discovery. But Jenny regains Mac and boards an airplane to take him back to Alaska and a friendly forest ranger, Jackson.

INT. BOARDING AREA - NIGHT

Charlie and Sarah watch the plane fly away.

                    CHARLIE
          I'd always heard a lot about you.

                    SARAH
          Let's go back to the hotel.

                    CHARLIE
          I've never been to Paris.

                    SARAH
          Now's a great time to visit.

                    CHARLIE
          Really. I may have some time off. I
          think Frank's going to recommend that I
          find...a new job. But that's okay. I'm
          in the mood for something new.

Sarah nods, and they walk down the hallway.

EXT. FAIRBANKS AIRPORT - NIGHT

Jenny and Mac sit, waiting until a truck pulls up.
People are staring at Jenny and Mac, who are still
in disguises.

> JENNY (to MAC)
> There he is. I know he can be trusted.

Jackson enters the airport. He smiles as he sees
them.

> JACKSON
> Hi. Welcome back. What do you want me
> to do?

INT. TRUCK - NIGHT

Jenny, Jackson and Mac drive slowly through the
night, along a brightly-lit night. They are in the
deep woods. Mac makes a noise. Jenny motions for
Jackson to stop the truck.

> JACKSON
> Here?

> JENNY
> Yeah. Mac knows.

They get out of the truck.

> JACKSON
> You're just going to let him go? Just
> like that?

> JENNY
> Yep.

> JACKSON
> What about your grant? Your proposal?

Jenny lifts Mac out of the truck and onto the
ground. The moonlight shines brightly and the horn
glistens in the light.

                    JENNY
          I know Mac will find me. When it's all
          set up. It's better this way.

                    JACKSON
          But your discovery?

                    JENNY
          I'm not going to let Mac die for my
          career. Besides, the discovery has
          already happened. Now we have to fig-
          ure out what it means. Mac doesn't
          have to stay around for that. He
          misses the others, his herd. They're
          doing something important.

Mac runs away into the woods, pausing for a moment,
and turning to look at Jenny, then vanishing into
the darkness.

                    JACKSON
          I could always see him, you know.

                    JENNY
          I know.

Jenny kisses Jackson.

EXT. BLUE TENTS, BASE CAMP - DAY

There's a new sign that reads "Top Secret USGS
Area. Trespassers will be prosecuted." There are
several blue tents situated in the woods. Jenny is
back at work. Around her, there are ten unicorns,
all engrossed in various activities. Jenny watches
one unicorn test water with its horn. Melissa
arrives carrying radio equipment. Alice pops out
of one tent. She smiles, surveying the scene.
Jackson sits nearby, watching.

21.
How to Structure a Teleplay

Viewing dramatic writing from a holistic, evolutionary stand-point, television is the latest and the greatest incarnation of the form. The concept of television drama is an interesting merging of fiction serials that appeared in weekly magazines in the early part of the 20th century with the dramatic form. These serials aired on the radio, and with the advent of camera technology moved to television.

Cliff-hangers used to be published daily and weekly in newspapers and magazines; people bought them eagerly to see what would happen next. Advertisers, of course, contributed to the publications' costs. This same concept was brought to life through radio and then television: serial dramas, with hooks that made people want to watch each week were created, and commercial sponsors paid to advertise dramas. The act breaks in television evolved to accommodate advertising. This put added pressure on the writer to capture an audience quickly; hang on to those viewers so they don't disappear to another channel during the breaks, and hang on to the viewers each week.

The current television market is very complex; again, I urge you to do further research and reading on the subject to become truly knowledgeable about how television writing works. Most of us feel more familiar with this form of dramatic writing than any other; I grew up on it, didn't you? Most of us do own a television, and the good news is you can study it every night in the comfort of your own home if you are so inclined. I urge you to look at it based on what you know about dramatic structure and see what your own analysis may yield regarding how to write an episode of a show.

Television shows are written by staffs — groups of writers working together on a regular basis. You can be hired on staff or on a one-shot, freelance basis. But you will need several sample "spec" scripts in order to break in and/or get an agent.

Here are some primary factors involved in writing for television:

SET LOCALES AND CHARACTERS

It is almost impossible to create a new series or pilot without a track record of working in television. Therefore, to start out, you will be writing samples of established shows on "spec" — (for free, speculative) to display your writing talent and solid knowledge of the form. These characters and locales have been created by someone else. You must show that you understand how the characters think and behave; you should not go outside of the established boundaries of character traits and settings already in place. There are parameters that you should adhere to.

ESTABLISH SITUATIONS QUICKLY

Because of the requirements of television writing as described above, it is necessary to show the essence of the action as quickly as possible; in plainer terms, set it up and get it going from the start. Your visual sense again is paramount. The stakes of characters should be clear and have import. Action is character; character is action, to bring up Aristotle again.

ACTS/HOOKS

The act form varies depending what form you are working in (see below). But every act should end with a hook, an intriguing, unresolved piece of action that compels the audience to sit through advertising to see what happens in the rest of your story.

PROTAGONIST/STAR

The episodes should be centered around the star. You know who the star is; make sure that you think of a storyline that revolves around him or her. Don't try to be original and write about a lesser character that personally fascinates you.

Should the star be changed the same way a protagonist in other dramatic forms is changed? Not much! Not in a spec script. Those kind of decisions will be made by the people who produce and staff the show. Remember, you're trying to demonstrate that you can write and that you understand the behavioral parameters of the show. Continuity is key; adhere to it.

DIFFERENT LENGTHS

Television is generally populated with three lengths of shows: the $1/2$ hour show (usually a comedy), the hour show (usually dramatic), and the 2-hour Movie of the Week (MOW).

The $1/2$ hour show ("sitcom" — short for situation comedy) is filled with regular characters and their life situations. Try to keep additional characters down to two for your spec, due to budgetary reasons. Also, stick to the sets that appear each week (let a staff writer do the extravagant thing). This type of show relies less on visual elements than character response. This is a two-act form and scenes run from three to five pages. Since these types of scripts use a double-spaced format, they run about forty-five pages total.

An hour show is broken into four acts. The acts runs about fifteen pages each, and each act is a separate unit with a crisis and climax all its own. Act Two must have the biggest climax because of the big commercial break that occurs there. The scripts are about 55 to 60 pages and run one minute per page. Scenes should be $2^1/2$ to 3 pages long.

The MOW follows the same invisible three-act format as described for screenplays, with the same lengths and requirements.

SHORT ITEMS

Here are some other structural concepts. A *teaser* is a short scene (one to three pages) often used to set up the show. A teaser is also a short scene (one to three pages) used to close some shows. You'll know if the show you're writing uses these devices or not. The long-running show, *Cheers*, used an opening teaser; the hit *Roseanne*, an (occasional) closing teaser.

A *runner* is an idea, motif, or device that "runs" like a thread throughout your script. These can be used in comedy and drama and are taken as a strong cohesive element that flows through the script.

WHAT SPEC SHOULD YOU WRITE?

Determining the spec you should prepare really depends on you and what you want to do. Whichever form you write in, make sure that you've viewed a specific show about six times to have a clear idea of what's going on and the established parameters.

FORMAT

The next two pages are examples of ½ hour format and 1 hour format. There are shows that differ from this because of the way they are shot: some ½ hour shows now use a film format, for example. You should check to see how the show you're going to write is shot, either by getting hold of a script, calling the show for information and ordering a sample script (that info is available through the *WGA Journal*), or going to the Writers Guild Library in Los Angeles to read sample scripts.

Finally, an informative book on accepted script format is available through the Writers Guild of America, East. Send your request for the *Professional Writer's Teleplay/Screenplay Guide* to Writers Guild of America, East, 555 West 57th Street, New York, NY 10019.

General Guidelines

½ hour: Lining up your printer on margin 0, scene descriptions start at 20 for the left margin and end at 70 for the right. Dialogue starts at 30 on the left and ends at 65 on the right. Character names start at 40 and page numbers go at 75.

All dialogue is double-spaced, all scene descriptions are capitalized, at the left margin. Scenes begin 15 spaces from the top of the page.

One-hour shows: The same as above except for dialogue information. Instead, dialogue is single-spaced.

The page number is four to six lines down from the top of the page. Act numbers are centered and are down about eleven lines with the title of the episode or MOW centered two spaces above. All scene settings start at the left margin. All description starts at the left margin, is single-spaced, and is written in lowercase. Double spaces are used between the scene settings and the description, and the character's name. Dialogue begins under the character's name. Triple space is used for a new scene.

½ HOUR SAMPLE

This is one example; shows vary. Obtain a sample of the show you want to write before you format it.

<u>ACT ONE</u>
<u>Scene 1</u>

<u>FADE IN</u>:

<u>INT. LOCATION OF YOUR CHOICE</u> - DAY
(List the characters in your scene)

IN CAPS, DESCRIBE THE ACTION YOUR SCENE BEGINS
WITH. DESCRIPTION IS SINGLE-SPACED BUT THE DIA-
LOGUE THAT FOLLOWS WILL BE DOUBLE-SPACED.

                    CHARACTER
          This is where the dialogue goes.
          It should be short and sweet.

                    CHARACTER
          When a character answers, it's done in
          the same format.

                    CHARACTER
          And so the scene continues.

(ANY MOVEMENT OR ACTION NEEDED IS INDICATED PAREN-
THETICALLY)

        CHARACTER
Let's get part of a scene going.

(DAN ENTERS)

        DAN
Okay….I'm home.

        MARJORIE (OS)
You're late.

(HE THROWS HIS BRIEFCASE AND JACKET ON THE COUCH)

ONE HOUR SAMPLE

        CHARACTER
Dialogue goes here.
Character names are in caps, of course.

        CHARACTER
Additional dialogue goes here.

If you want to add some description of action or
reaction, you can add it anywhere. Double-space
after description.

        CHARACTER
The format continues in this manner.
You can also put in small movements for
the character who is speaking, like
(she shakes her head) and continue with
the dialogue.

Description is given single-spaced. Use a clean,
terse style that will clearly show the action.

        CHARACTER
More dialogue as the scene continues or
ends. This page will continue with a
mini-scene.

INT. KITCHEN - LATER THAT NIGHT

Frank opens the door and quietly tiptoes across the
kitchen. Suddenly the lights flash on. Karen is
waiting for him, holding a gun.

                    KAREN
          Look what the cat dragged in.

                    FRANK
          Karen. I was going to call you--

                    KAREN
          Too late now.

She walks around him in a circle, eyeing his
clothes. Frank watches her nervously.

                    KAREN
          You're kind of a mess.

22.
Marketing for the Screen

Once you have a finished script, you will want to get it seen by as many industry professionals as possible. This will usually happen in two ways: through an agent or through contacts you make yourself.

If you live outside of Los Angeles or New York, you will have a difficult time marketing your screenplay/teleplay. The reasons for this are obvious: people want to meet you after they've read your work. It's all about meetings — do they want to work with you? What are your other ideas? You have to meet lots of people in order to work in this industry, and if you live outside of the immediate area, it makes it a bit more difficult. Also, for television, to be on staff, clearly you'd need to live nearby. Even on a freelance basis, you need to take meetings.

I know some writers who fly in and out of town for meetings but live somewhere else. They are either "famous, well-established" writers, or people who built relationships with agents through some other means: winning awards, knowing someone who gave someone a script, etc. Anyway, although it's possible, it's unusual and you should know that from the outset, especially for television.

AGENTS

Getting an agent or some sort of entertainment representative is absolutely necessary. You need an agent in order to have your work submitted to people who make decisions. A few places will take unsolicited scripts, but you must sign a release form and it usually means your stuff is buried somewhere being read by a reader, who is paid to write an evaluation of it. Your work will read by readers anyway, but agents are the normal channel for submission; they have working rapports with people who buy scripts and hire writers. You're taken seriously if you have an agent.

How do you get an agent? It helps if someone recommends you. But no matter what, you must submit samples of your work. Write to the Agency Department of the Writers Guild of America, East at 555 West 57th Street, New York, NY 10019 (212) 245-6180 or West at 8955 Beverly Blvd., West Hollywood, CA 90048 (213) 550-1000. The Guild offices have a list of agents who represent all writers working in film and television. Sometimes they can tell you agents who are looking for new clients.

Write a query letter or call these agents and ask if you can send along your script. Include a self-addressed, stamped envelope to get the script back after they're finished with it.

CONTACTS

Another way to get an agent or a potential sale is through professional contacts. I can't stress the value of contacts enough. Network. Meet people who work in the industry. Talk to people about writing and about what you want to do. Put out a general alert. Especially, talk to other writers. Take classes, go to special events about writing. Get a job in the industry if you'd like to really learn how things work.

Other writers are an excellent resource on everything you're interested in. Writers hire other writers; writers know agents, producers, development executives, etc. Try to meet other writers. Ask them nicely to read your work. Truly, writers are a generous breed — it's amazing how many of them appreciate talent and, of course, they seek it professionally. Get to know as many as you can. Join writers' groups.

The trade journals are another source of general marketing information: read *Variety* and *Hollywood Reporter* to find out who is doing what in the industry.

WRITERS GUILD

The Writers Guild exists to represent all writers for collective bargaining in movie, TV, and radio. It doesn't employ writers, instruct writers, or submit material. It does have support services. Of crucial importance is its script registration procedure, as mentioned in Chapter 16. It also publishes the *WGAW Journal*, available to nonmembers at $40 a year or $5 per issue. The *Journal* lists contact submission information on current weekly prime-time television shows. There are lots of different ways your work can be purchased, optioned, etc. The Guild's rules represent the official procedure in these instances. I encourage you to explore the business side of writing deals in order to make the best kinds of decisions.

In order to become a member of the WGA, you must complete twelve units of credit under contract or employment or upon the sale or licensing of previously unpublished, un-produced literary or dramatic material. This work must be done with a company or other entity that is signatory to the applicable WGA Collective Bargaining Agreement and must be within jurisdiction of the Guild as provided for in its contracts. The twelve units must be accumulated within the preceding two years of application. There is an initiation fee of $1,500.

AWARDS

There are organizations that offer awards for first-time writers for the screen: the Nichols Award and the Leslie Stevens Award are two such prizes that get attention in the industry. For information, contact the Academy of Motion Pictures in Los Angeles.

Other awards are possible through film schools. If you are enrolled in a university, your work may be eligible for competitions if your school has a film department. Check with the department to see what's available.

23.
The Future of Writing in
These Mediums

I hope you've learned a lot from this process; I especially hope you're excited about theatrical writing forms. One thing all three types have in common is the word "play": play, screenplay, teleplay. Writing for the dramatic form is "play" making. Be playful.

As I'm sure you've gathered by now, I'm on a mission to draw attention to the dramatic form in our highly technical and complicated culture. I believe these works, in addition to entertaining us, will constantly reflect the changing lives and behavior of human beings. Drama will always amplify and attempt to explain the evolution of the human condition, and it is this presentational interaction with others that will ensure its continued existence as an art form. We want to examine ourselves in a social arena. We need to laugh and cry together. We want to feel each other's hearts.

I think that all three dramatic forms will continue to feed and affect each other from an aesthetic standpoint: a sort of symbiosis and spawning will continue to occur as specific elements cross back and forth between the three. Elements from the cinema continue to spill back into theater, film techniques into television, etc.

Also, even more exciting, is the continued possibility of fusion with other forms. In the way that film came from theater and photography, and television was based on the ideas of serialized short stories coming to life, so the artistic evolution of drama will continue to surprise and grow, based on synthesis with forms that may not have been developed yet. Because drama is a living, breathing art form, it will grow and change, always keeping pace with human nature and ingenuity.

How does that affect you and your future? I think you may have a big part in it. I challenge you to be original, to change the face of drama, whether you write for stage or screen —

change it to reflect the world as you know it now, and what you foresee as important for the future. Contemplate the audience; connect with them in new ways, innovative ways, ways they can't get anywhere else. Fail a few times if you need to, but experiment. Explore.

Make a contribution to an art form that's alive, waiting to be "played" with.

Students often ask me at the end of writing courses if they should become writers. When I first started teaching, I would innocently discuss the possibilities with each individual. I'd go over the options of making money, the specifics of the "writing life," and try to give them some rather depressing but true statistics about how difficult it is to "make it" as a writer.

After a while, however, I began to realize that none of that information mattered. I thought back to my own journey on the "writing" road. I must have had at least fifty teachers tell me what a good writer I was, through the years. Other writers were very generous in their comments of encouragement to me. I won awards. I had a lot of outside support.

But none of those things enabled me to be a writer. It isn't an external decision; it's an internal one. *I* wanted to write. It didn't matter who told me I could or should or couldn't or shouldn't (and believe me, there were a few people who tried to discourage me). It didn't matter that I would be broke much of the time. I wanted to write. It was as simple as that.

And so I close by answering the inevitable question, "Should you pursue writing?" It's all in your hands. If you have the desire, you can develop the craft and nurture your own talent. If you want to do it, do it passionately.

In 1980, William Saroyan said to me: "No matter how fast you write, write faster. And never listen to anyone."

Now I say to you: Listen to your heart. If it gives you joy, do it. Do it now and don't look back. If you must look, look ahead.

Appendix 1. Theaters

Actors Alliance Theatre Co.
30800 Evergreen Road
Southfield, MI 48076
(313) 642-1326

The Actors' Company of
  Pennsylvania
Box 1153
Lancaster, PA 17603
(717) 397-1251

Actors Theatre of Louisville
316 West Main Street
Louisville, KY 40202
(502) 584-1265

A.D. Players
2710 West Alabama Street
Houston, TX 77098
(713) 526-2721

Alabama Shakespeare Festival
1 Festival Drive
Montgomery, AL 36117
(205) 272-1640

Alley Theatre
615 Texas Avenue
Houston, TX 77002
(713) 228-9341

Alliance Theatre Company
1280 Peachtree Street NE
Atlanta, GA 30309
(404) 898-1132

American Conservatory Theater
450 Geary Street
San Francisco, CA 94102
(415) 749-2200

American Place Theatre
111 W. 46th Street
New York, NY 10036
(212) 840-2960

American Repertory Theatre
64 Brattle Street
Cambridge, MA 02138
(617) 495-2668

American Stage
Box 1560
St. Petersburg, FL 33731
(813) 823-1600

American Theatre Co.
Box 1265
Tulsa, OK 74101
(918) 747-9494

Arena Players Repertory Co. of
  Long Island
296 Farmingdale Road
East Farmingdale, NY 11735
(516) 293-0674

Arena Stage
6th and Maine Avenue, SW
Washington, DC 20024
(202) 554-9066

Arizona Theatre Company
56 West Congress, Box 1631
Tucson, AZ 85702
(602) 884-8210

Arkansas Repertory Theatre
Box 110
Little Rock, AR 72203
(501) 378-0405

Arrow Rock Lyceum Theatre
Main Street
Arrow Rock, MO 65320
(816) 837-3311

Barter Theatre
Box 867
Abingdon, VA 24210
(703) 628-2281

Berkeley Repertory Theatre
2025 Addison Street
Berkeley, CA 94704
(415) 841-6108

The Berkshire Public Theatre
Box 860
Pittsfield, MA 01202
(413) 445-4631

Bilingual Foundation of the Arts
421 North Avenue 19
Los Angeles, CA 90031
(213) 225-4044

Bloomsburg Theatre Ensemble
Box 66
Bloomsburg, PA 17815
(717) 784-5530

The Body Politic Theatre
2261 North Lincoln Avenue
Chicago, IL 60614
(312) 348-7901

Brass Tacks Theatre
401 Third Street N, Suite 450
Minneapolis, MN 55401
(612) 341-8207

Clarence Brown Theatre Co.
UT Box 8450
Knoxville, TN 37996
(615) 974-6011

California Theatre Center
Box 2007
Sunnyvale, CA 94087
(408) 245-2979

Capital Repertory Co.
Box 399
Albany, NY 12201
(518) 462-4531

The Cast Theatre
804 North El Centro Avenue
Hollywood, CA 90038
(213) 462-9872

Center Stage
700 North Calvert Street
Baltimore, MD 21202
(301) 685-3200

Changing Scene
1527 1/2 Champa Street
Denver, CO 80202
(303) 893-5775

Charlotte Repertory Theatre
345 N. College Street, Suite 211
Charlotte, NC 28202
(704) 375-4796

Chelsea Stage
441 W. 26th Street
New York, NY 10001
(212) 645-4940

Children's Theatre Co.
2400 Third Avenue S.
Minneapolis, MN 55404
(612) 874-0500

Circle Repertory Co.
161 Avenue of the Americas
New York, NY 10013
(212) 691-3210

Circle Theatre
2015 South 60th Street
Omaha, NE 68106
(402) 553-4715

Cleveland Public Theatre
6415 Detroit Avenue
Cleveland, OH 44102
(216) 631-2727

Colony Studio Theatre
1944 Riverside Drive
Los Angeles, CA 90039

Company One Theatre (one acts)
30 Arbor Street S
Hartford, CT 06106

A Contemporary Theatre
100 West Roy Street
Seattle, WA 98119
(206) 285-3220

Creede Repertory Theatre
Box 269
Creede, CO 81130
(719) 658-2541

The Cricket Theatre
1407 Nicollet Avenue
Minneapolis, MN 55403
(612) 871-3763

Crossroads Theatre Co.
320 Memorial Pkwy.
New Brunswick, NJ 08901
(201) 249-5625

Delaware Theatre Co.
Box 516
Wilmington, DE 19899
(302) 594-1104

Dell'Arte Players Co.
Box 816
Blue Lake, CA 95525
(707) 668-5663

Denver Center Theatre Co.
1050 13th Street
Denver, CO 80204
(303) 893-4200

Detroit Repertory Theatre
13103 Woodrow Wilson Avenue
Detroit, MI 48238
(313) 868-1347

East West Players
4424 Santa Monica Blvd.
Los Angeles, CA 90029
(213) 660-0366

Empire State Institute for the
    Performing Arts
1400 Washington Avenue,
PAC266
Albany, NY 12222
(518) 442-5399

Empty Space Theatre
Box 1748
Seattle, WA 98111
(206) 587-3737

Ensemble Studio Theatre
549 W. 52nd Street
New York, NY 10019
(212) 581-9603

Ensemble Theatre of Cincinnati
1127 Vine Street
Cincinnati, OH 45210
(513) 421-3556

Eureka Theatre Co.
2730 16th Street
San Francisco, CA 94103
(415) 558-9811

First Stage Milwaukee
929 North Water Street
Milwaukee, WI 53202
(414) 273-7121

Florida Studio Theatre
1241 North Palm Avenue
Sarasota, FL 34236
(813) 366-9017

FMT
Box 07147
Milwaukee, WI 53207
(414) 271-8484

George Street Playhouse
9 Livingston Avenue
New Brunswick, NJ 08901
(201) 846-2895

GeVa Theatre
75 Woodbury Blvd.
Rochester, NY 14607
(716) 232-1366

Gloucester Stage Company
267 East Main Street
Gloucester, MA 01930
(508) 281-4099

Great North American
  History Theatre
30 East 10th Street
St. Paul, MN 55101
(612) 292-4323

Guthrie Theatre
725 Vineland Place
Minneapolis, MN 55403
(612) 347-1100

Hartford Stage Company
50 Church Street
Hartford, CT 06103
(203) 525-5601

Hippodrome State Theatre
25 SE 2nd Place
Gainesville, FL 32601
(904) 373-5968

Honolulu Theatre for Youth
2846 Ualena Street
Honolulu, HI 96819
(808) 839-9885

Horizons: Theatre from A
  Woman's Perspective
1041 Wisconsin Avenue NW
Washington, DC 20007
(202) 342-5503

Illinois Theatre Center
400A Lakewood Blvd.
Park Forest, IL 60466
(312) 481-3510

Illusion Theater
528 Hennepin Avenue, Suite 704
Minneapolis, MN 55403
(612) 339-4944

Indiana Repertory Theatre
140 West Washington Street
Indianapolis, IN 46204
(317) 635-5277

Intar Hispanic American Arts
  Center
Box 788
New York, NY 10108
(212) 695-6134

Intiman Theatre Company
Box 19645
Seattle, WA 98109
(206) 626-0775

Jewish Repertory Theatre
344 East 14th Street
New York, NY 10003
(212) 674-7200

L.A. Theatre Works
681 Venice Blvd.
Venice, CA 90291
(213) 827-0808

Lifeline Theatre
6912 North Glenwood
Chicago, IL 60626
(312) 761-4477

Long Island Stage
Box 9001
Rockville Centre, NY 11571
(516) 546-4600

Madison Repertory Theatre
211 State Street
Madison, WI 53703
(608) 256-0029

Magic Theatre
Fort Mason Center Bldg. D
San Francisco, CA 94123
(415) 441-8001

Main Street Theatre
2540 Times Blvd.
Houston, TX 77005
(713) 524-3662

Manhattan Punch Line Theatre
410 W. 16th Street, 3rd Floor
New York, NY 10036
(212) 239-0827

Manhattan Theatre Club
453 W. 16th Street
New York, NY 10011
(212) 645-5590

Mark Taper Forum
135 N. Grand Avenue
Los Angeles, CA 90012
(213) 972-7353

Merrimack Repertory Theatre
Box 228
Lowell, MA 01853
(508) 454-6324

Metro Theatre Co.
524 Trinity Avenue
St. Louis, MO 63130
(314) 727-3552

Mill Mountain Theatre
Center in the Square
One Market Square
Roanoke, VA 24011
(703) 342-5730

Missouri Repertory Theatre
4949 Cherry Street
Kansas City, MO 64110
(816) 363-4541

Mixed Blood Theatre Co.
1501 South 4th Street
Minneapolis, MN 55454
(612) 338-0937

Moving Target Theatre Co.
Box 225794
Dallas, TX 75222
(214) 979-2599

National Jewish Theater
5050 W. Church Street
Skokie, IL 60077
(312) 675-2200

Nebraska Theatre Caravan
6915 Cass Street
Omaha, NE 68132
(402) 553-4890

New American Theatre
118 North Main Street
Rockford, IL 61101
(815) 964-9454

New Jersey Shakespeare
Festival
Drew University, Rte. 24
Madison, NJ 07940
(201) 408-3278

New Mexico Repertory Theatre
Box 789
Albuquerque, NM 87103
(505) 243-4577

New Stage Theatre
1100 Carlisle Street
Jackson, MS 39202
(601) 948-3533

New Theatre
Box 650696
Miami, FL 33265
(305) 595-4260

New Theatre of Brooklyn
465 Dean Street
Brooklyn, NY 11217
(718) 230-3366

New York Shakespeare Festival
Public Theatre
425 Lafayette Street
New York, NY 10003
(212) 598-7129

New York Theatre Workshop
220 West 42nd Street,
18th Floor
New York, NY 10036
(212) 302-7737

Northlight Theatre
2300 Green Bay Road
Evanston, IL 60201
(708) 869-7732

Oakland Ensemble Theater
1428 Alice Street, Suite 289
Oakland, CA 94612
(415) 763-7774

Odyssey Theatre Ensemble
2055 South Sepulveda Blvd.
Los Angeles, CA 90025
(213) 477-2055

Old Creamery Theatre Co.
Box 160
Garrison, IA 52229
(319) 477-3925

Old Globe Theatre
Box 2171
San Diego, CA 92112
(619) 231-1941

Omaha Magic Theatre
1417 Farnam Street
Omaha, NE 68102
(402) 346-1227

The Open Eye
270 W. 89th Street
New York, NY 10024
(212) 769-4143

Oregon Shakespeare Festival
Box 158
Ashland, OR 97520
(503) 482-2111

Organic Theatre Co.
3319 North Street
Chicago, IL 60657
(312) 327-2427

164

Pan Asian Repertory Theatre
47 Great Jones Street
New York, NY 10012
(212) 505-5655

Paper Mill Playhouse
Brookside Drive
Millburn, NJ 07041
(201) 379-3636

PCPA Theaterfest
Box 1700
Santa Maria, CA 93456
(805) 928-7731

Pennsylvania Stage Co.
837 Linden Street
Allentown, PA 18101
(215) 434-8570

Penumbra Theatre Co.
Martin Luther King Bldg.
270 North Kent Street
St. Paul, MN 55102
(612) 224-4601

Perseverance Theatre
914 3rd Street
Douglas, AK 99824
(907) 364-2421

Philadelphia Drama Guild
Robert Morris Bldg.
100 North 17th Street
Philadelphia, PA 19103
(215) 563-7530

Philadelphia Theatre Co.
The Bourse Bldg., Suite 735
21 South 5th Street
Philadelphia, PA 19106
(215) 592-8333

Pioneer Theatre Co.
University of Utah
Salt Lake City, UT 84112
(801) 581-6356

Playhouse on the Square
51 South Cooper Street
Memphis, TN 38104
(901) 725-0776

Playmakers Repertory Co.
CB# 3235 Graham Memorial
Bldg.
Chapel Hill, NC 27599
(919) 962-1122

Playwrights Horizons
416 W. 42nd Street
New York, NY 10036
(212) 564-1235

Portland Repertory Theatre
2 World Trade Center
25 SW Salmon Street
Portland, OR 97204
(503) 224-4491

Portland Stage Co.
Box 1458
Portland, ME 04104
(207) 774-1043

Puerto Rican Traveling Theatre
Box 148
330 W. 42nd Street
New York, NY 10036
(212) 354-1293

Quaigh Theatre
205 W. 89th Street
New York, NY 10024
(212) 223-2547

Remains Theatre
1300 West Belmont Avenue
Chicago, IL 60657
(312) 549-7725

Repertorio Espanol
138 East 27th Street
New York, NY 10016
(212) 889-2850

Repertory Theatre of St. Louis
Box 28030
St. Louis, MO 63119
(314) 968-7340

Rites and Reason
Box 1148
Brown University
Providence, RI 02901
(401) 863-3558

Roadside Theater
306 Madison Street
Whitesburg, KY 41858
(606) 633-0108

Roundabout Theatre Co.
100 East 17th Street
New York, NY 10003
(212) 420-1360

Sacramento Theatre Co.
1419 H Street
Sacramento, CA 95814
(916) 446-7501

Salt Lake Acting Co.
168 West 500 N.
Salt Lake City, UT 84103
(801) 363-0526

Saltworks Theatre Co.
The Design Center
5001 Baum Blvd.
Pittsburgh, PA 15213
(412) 687-8883

San Diego Repertory Theatre
79 Horton Plaza
San Diego, CA 92101
(619) 231-3586

San Jose Repertory Theatre
Box 2399
San Jose, CA 95109
(408) 294-7595

Seattle Group Theatre
3940 Brooklyn Avenue NE
Seattle, WA 98105
(206) 685-4969

Seattle Repertory Theatre
155 Mercer Street
Seattle, WA 98109
(206) 443-2210

Second Stage Theatre
Box 1807
Ansonia Theatre
New York, NY 10023
(212) 787-8302

Snowmass/Aspen Repertory
Theatre
Box 6275
Snowmass Village, CO 81615
(303) 923-2618

Source Theatre Co.
1835 14th Street NW
Washington, DC 20009
(202) 462-1073

South Coast Repertory
Box 2197
Costa Mesa, CA 92628
(714) 957-2602

South Jersey Regional Theatre
Bay Avenue
Somers Point, NJ 08244
(609) 653-0553

Stage One: The Louisville
Children's Theatre
425 West Market Street
Louisville, KY 40202
(502) 589-5946

Stage West
Box 2587
Fort Worth, TX 76113
(817) 332-6265

Steppenwolf Theatre Co.
2851 North Halsted Street
Chicago, IL 60657
(312) 472-4515

Storefront Theatre
213 Southwest Ash Street,
Suite 209
Portland, OR 97204
(503) 224-9598

Studio Arena Theatre
710 Main Street
Buffalo, NY 14202
(716) 856-8025

Studio Theatre
1333 P Street NW
Washington, DC 20005
(202) 232-7267

Tacoma Actors Guild
1323 South Yakima Avenue
Tacoma, WA 98405
(206) 272-3107

Tennessee Repertory Theatre
427 Chestnut Street
Nashville, TN 37203
(615) 244-4878

Theatre De La Jeune Lune
Box 25170
Minneapolis, MN 55458
(612) 332-3968

Theater for the New City
155 First Avenue
New York, NY 10003
(212) 254-1109

Theatre IV
7 $\frac{1}{2}$ W. Marshall Street
Richmond, VA 23220
(804) 783-1688

Theatre Project Co.
634 North Grand Avenue,
Suite 10-H
St. Louis, MO 63103
(314) 531-1315

Theatre Rhinoceros
2926 16th Street
San Francisco, CA 94103
(415) 552-4100

Theatre X
Box 92206
Milwaukee, WI 53202
(414) 278-0555

Theatreworks
1305 Middlefield Road
Palo Alto, CA 94301
(415) 323-8311

Theatreworks/USA
890 Broadway
New York, NY 10003
(212) 677-5959

Touchstone Theatre
321 East 4th Street
Bethlehem, PA 18015
(215) 867-1689

Trinity Repertory Co.
201 Washington Street
Providence, RI 02903
(401) 521-1100

Undermain Theatre
Box 141166
Dallas, TX 75214
(214) 748-3082

Victory Gardens Theatre
2257 North Lincoln Avenue
Chicago, IL 60614
(312) 549-5788

Vineyard Theatre
108 East 15th Street
New York, NY 10003
(212) 353-3366

West Coast Ensemble
Box 38728
Los Angeles, CA 90038
(213) 871-8673

Wisdom Bridge Theatre
1559 West Howard Street
Chicago, IL 60626
(312) 743-0486

The Women's Project and
    Productions
220 W. 42nd Street, 18th Floor
New York, NY 10036
(212) 382-2750

Woolly Mammoth Theatre Co.
1401 Church Street, NW
Washington, DC 20005
(202) 393-3939

Worcester Foothills Theatre
    Company
074 Worcester Center
Worcester, MA 01608
(508) 754-3314

Yale Repertory Theatre
Box 1903A
Yale Station
New Haven, CT 06520
(203) 432-1560

Appendix 2.
Recommended Reading

If you are really interested in dramatic writing, you will want to learn as much as you can, as quickly as possible. In addition to viewing as much theater, film, and television as you can, read as many books as possible on the form that interests you the most.

Often, writing students express confusion to me about hearing conflicting things about writing: one professor tells you one thing, another writer will say something else. Discover the philosophy that suits you or maybe you'll want to do as I did: develop your own.

Convinced yet? Go to a library — all writers end up there sooner or late. Go to a bookstore — all writers want to end up there sooner or later.

Dramatic Structure

The Art of Dramatic Writing by Lajos Egri. Simon and Schuster, 1979.

The Art of the Playwright: Creating the Magic of Theatre by William Packard. Paragon Publishers, 1987.

Characters in Action by Marshall Cassady. University Press, New York, 1984.

Composing Drama for Stage and Screen by Stanley Vincent Longman, Allyn and Bacon, 1986.

How to Write a Play by Raymond Hull. Writer's Digest Books, 1983.

Playwriting: How to Write for the Theater by Bernard Grebanier. Barnes and Noble, 1961.

Playwriting: The Structure of Action by Sam Smiley. Prentice-Hall, Inc., 1971.

The Playwright's Handbook by Frank Pike and Thomas Dunn. Plume Books, 1985.

Stage Marketing

Dramatists Sourcebook, published by Theatre Communications Group. 355 Lexington Avenue, New York, NY 10017. The best book on marketing for playwrights; complete listing

Playwrights' Companion, a submission guide to theaters and contests in the USA. Feedback Books, available through Samuel French Trade, 7623 Sunset Blvd., Hollywood, CA 90046.

Writer's Market, Writer's Digest Books, Cincinnati. Annual updates on marketing information published.

Film Structure

The Elements of Screenwriting: A Guide for Film and Television Writing by Irwin Blacker. Collier Books, 1986.

How to Write a Movie in 21 Days by Viki King. Harper and Row, 1988.

Screenplay by Syd Field. Dell, 1984.

Screenwriter's Workbook by Syd Field. Dell, 1988.

Screenplays

(Even though they're usually published in a shooting script format, read some classic screenplays.)

Best American Screenplays edited by Sam Thomas. Crown Publishers, 1986.

The Complete Guide to Standard Script Formats, Part 1, The Screenplay by Cole and Haag. CMC Publishing, 1980.

Television Structure

The Elements of Screenwriting: A Guide for Film and Television Writing by Irwin Blacker. Collier Books, 1986.

Write for Television by Madeline DiMaggio. Prentice-Hall, 1990.

General Writing Inspiration

Becoming a Writer by Dorothea Brande. Jeremy P. Tarcher, 1981.

If You Want to Write by Brenda Ueland. Graywolf Press, 1938.

Writing Down the Bones by Natalie Goldberg. Shambhala Publishing, 1986.

Glossary of Dramatic Terms

ACT — A unit of dramatic action composed of several scenes. Theater: about an hour's worth of material. Film: Act 1, about 30 pages; Act 2, about 60 more pages; Act 3, about 30 pages. TV: varies depending on the length of form you're writing in — about 12 minutes of material.

ACTION — What happens in a scene. Through conflict, there is motion and movement. Something changes through a confrontation with another person, an event, etc.

ACTION POINT — The point of action where your scene/script begins: your character should already be in motion; begin on the cusp of the middle of movement.

ACTORS — The artists who bring your script to life by acting out the roles, moving through your story. It is their presence, and their link to the audience, that makes drama a three-dimensional form.

ANTAGONIST — The counter-hero, the character that opposes your protagonist for excellent reasons and sets up a series of obstacles for your protagonist to overcome. Often "understood" in modern stage plays; usually visible in screen forms.

BACKSTORY — See EXPOSITION.

BEAT — The smallest unit of dramatic action — moments of exchange that escalate conflict in a scene. Beats are the building block units of scene; they escalate to result in a climax — the most powerful moment in any scene.

CHARACTER — The people who bring your story to life; principally of concern to the writer are: the main character, the allies of the main characters, and the antagonist. Character is linked to action; human nature is revealed through behavior. How your characters act and what they say reveal who they are. Show character, don't tell it.

CLIMAX — Climax is two things: the most powerful part of any scene and, in traditional structure, the biggest moment in your script, after which falling action (denouement) occurs. When two opposing forces meet, a climax results as the action escalates. Character transformation occurs as a result of the climax.

COMEDY — A script in which transformation occurs and the ending is happy. It should be full of humor.

CONFLICT—When two opposing forces meet, there is conflict. When there are obstacles, there is conflict. When a character is challenged to a new level, there is conflict. With action, conflict is a necessary dynamic of dramatic writing; through behavioral interaction with obstacles, characters change.

DENOUEMENT (or FALLING ACTION) — After the biggest climax of your script, there is a period of falling action, when results of the biggest event in your script are played out. In falling action, protagonist transformation is revealed.

DESCRIPTION — The part of a script for stage or screen that depicts physical elements, describing how things look. Keep it clean and simple but direct and visual.

DESIGNER — An artist responsible for designing technical/ physical elements of your script — again, bringing to life your ideas and making your work a three-dimensional form.

DIALOGUE — What the characters say; speech. It should sound natural and "character-specific." Remember that we rarely speak in complete sentences or thoughts.

DIRECTOR — The artist responsible for mounting a script for performance on either stage or screen.

DRAMATIC WRITING — The art and craft of writing in a three-dimensional form; work written to be performed in front of an audience.

EXPOSITION—Backstory, history, what has happened before the action in your script. Elements of character and story that affect why a character is reacting a certain way to the current situation.

FALLING ACTION — See DENOUEMENT.

FLASHBACK—A time sequence that occurs in the past; going back in time to a previous, relevant point of a character's life.

HOOK — An intriguing action occurring at the end of an act, in any dramatic form, that propels the action forward and compels the audience to keep watching, to come back for more. It happens before an intermission, before a commercial, or on the cusp of screenplay acts.

INTERMISSION — A break in performance, in between acts in the theater. People frolic in lobbies during these brief pauses.

LIGHTING — The way we see your script; lights used to bring the actors and action into the visual realm of the audience/camera.

PLAY — A script written for the stage.

PLOT — The sequence of events that occur in your script, starring your protagonist. At the end of the series of events, your protagonist is changed, transformed, different than before it all began.

PROPERTIES (PROPS) — The physical objects that your actors use in bringing your script to life. They may be small or large items, but they are used by characters in some meaningful way.

PROTAGONIST — The leading character of your script ... who the story is about ... who it all happens to, the hero or heroine, the one who transforms.

SCENE — A small unit of dramatic action in which *something happens* through conflict and resulting action. Tension propels scenes forward. Length of a scene varies depending on the form you're writing in. Stage: can be any length. Screen: 3-5 pages.

SETTING — Where your script takes place: locations, locales. The arena your action happens in.

SCREENPLAY — A script written for film.

SOUND — The aural elements of your script.

SPECTACLE — The big, visual picture that you, as a dramatic writer, must strive to present throughout your script no matter what form you are writing in. Think visually. Think of the stage or screen as a canvas. Dazzle an audience with visuals.

STORY — The same as plot: the list of the events of your script.

TELEPLAY — A script written for television.

THEME — The point of your writing, the message and passion behind your ideas.

TONE — The intention or feeling through which you tell your story and present your ideas, giving the audience a sense of your "take" on the story: do you want us to laugh, cry, both?

TOPIC — The general subject area of your story.

TRAGEDY — A script with a sad ending through which a character undergoes a grave catharsis; usually ends with death.

TRANSFORMATION — Change. Your plot is designed with this change in mind for your protagonist. Other characters may change, too, but your protagonist *must*; otherwise, why did your story occur?

TREATMENT — An outline of the scenes in your screenplay or teleplay with a paragraph describing each.

VOICE — The unique element of your writing: only you can tell this story in your way. The combination of all ingredients of dramatic form culminate in precious vision: yours, writing now, writing today.

WRITER'S BLOCK — A dreaded "disease" that writers use to psyche themselves out from writing.

Index

Index